Quality by Design in Pharmaceutical Industry

Quality by Design in Pharmaceutical Industry

Dr. V. Venkateswarlu
Managing Director,
Neuheit Pharma Technologies Private Limited,
Plot no 9, Block A,
ALEAP Green Industrial Estates (A-GRIP).
Nandigama Village (G.P.), Mandal- Patancheru
District- Sangareddy, Telangana, India
PIN CODE- 502319

PharmaMed Press
An imprint of BSP Books Pvt. Ltd.

PharmaMed Press™
An imprint of BSP Books Pvt. Ltd.
4-4-309/316, Giriraj Lane,
Sultan Bazar, Hyderabad - 500 001,
Telangana, India.

Quality by Design in Pharmaceutical Industry
by V. Venkateswarlu

Published by

Pharma Med PRESS
An Imprint of BSP Books Pvt. Ltd.

™ **PharmaMed Press**
An imprint of BSP Books Pvt. Ltd.
4-4-309/316, Giriraj Lane, Sultan Bazar,
Hyderabad - 500 001, Telangana, India.
Phone: 040-23445688
E-mail: info@pharmamedpress.net
www.bspbooks.net/www.pharmamedpress.net

ISBN: 978-93-47311-40-6 (Hardback)

Preface

Quality by Design (QbD) has transformed the way pharmaceutical products are conceived, developed, manufactured, and continuously improved. Moving beyond the traditional paradigm of quality being tested into products, QbD emphasizes a scientific, risk-based, and proactive approach in which quality is built in from the earliest stages of development. This shift is not merely regulatory in nature; it reflects a deeper evolution in pharmaceutical thinking—one that integrates product understanding, process knowledge, and lifecycle management into a unified framework for delivering safe, effective, and high-quality medicines.

This book, "Quality by Design in Pharmaceutical Industry", has been written to bridge the gap between regulatory expectations, scientific principles, and practical implementation. It aims to serve as a comprehensive resource for students, researchers, formulation scientists, process engineers, quality professionals, and regulatory affairs specialists who seek to understand and apply QbD concepts across the pharmaceutical product lifecycle. From target product profile definition and critical quality attribute identification to design space establishment, control strategies, and continuous improvement, the book provides both conceptual clarity and practical insight.

Recognizing the interdisciplinary nature of QbD, this book integrates perspectives from pharmaceutics, analytical sciences, process engineering, statistics, and quality risk management. Special emphasis is placed on the application of tools such as Design of Experiments (DoE), process analytical technology (PAT), and risk assessment methodologies, supported by real-world case studies and industry-relevant examples. These illustrations are intended to demystify QbD and demonstrate its applicability to small molecules, complex generics, biologics, and advanced dosage forms.

In an era of increasing product complexity, globalized supply chains, and heightened regulatory scrutiny, QbD offers a robust framework for achieving regulatory flexibility, operational efficiency, and sustainable product quality. Regulatory initiatives from agencies worldwide, including ICH guidelines such as Q8, Q9, Q10, and Q12, underscore the growing importance of QbD as a cornerstone of modern pharmaceutical development and manufacturing. This book aligns closely with these guidelines while maintaining a strong focus on practical implementation in both research and industrial settings.

It is our hope that this book will not only enhance technical understanding but also inspire a quality-centric mindset—one that encourages innovation, scientific rigor, and continuous learning. By fostering a systematic approach to product and process development, "Quality by Design in Pharmaceutical Industry" aspires to contribute to the ultimate goal of the pharmaceutical profession: delivering high-quality medicines that consistently meet patient needs and improve global health.

-Author

Acknowledgements

The successful completion of this book would not have been possible without the encouragement, support, and contributions of many individuals and organizations to whom I am deeply grateful.

I sincerely acknowledge the scientists and professionals at Neuheit Pharma Technologies for their scientific rigor, collaborative spirit, and shared commitment to advancing quality-driven pharmaceutical development. Their discussions, insights, and practical perspectives have helped reinforce the real-world relevance of Quality by Design (QbD) principles presented in this book.

I extend my special gratitude to my colleagues and mentors at Dr. Reddy's Laboratories, where I had the privilege of championing and implementing Quality by Design concepts across pharmaceutical development and manufacturing activities. The progressive culture, openness to innovation, and strong emphasis on science- and risk-based decision-making at Dr. Reddy's played a pivotal role in shaping my understanding and conviction that QbD is not merely a regulatory expectation, but a powerful enabler of sustainable quality and excellence.

I also express my sincere appreciation to Pharma Book Syndicate, Hyderabad, for their professional support, cooperation, and commitment in bringing this book to publication. Their efforts in editorial coordination, production, and dissemination have contributed significantly to the timely and effective presentation of this work to the scientific and industrial community.

I am profoundly thankful to my family for their unwavering support and encouragement throughout this journey. My heartfelt appreciation goes to my son Vamshi Krishna, my daughter Priyanka, and my daughter-in-law Yogitha, whose patience, motivation, and belief in my work provided constant strength and inspiration. Their understanding and encouragement made it possible for me to dedicate the time and focus required to complete this book.

I am also grateful to the wider scientific, academic, and industrial community whose published research, regulatory guidance, and shared experiences continue to advance the field of pharmaceutical quality. Finally, I acknowledge all those—named and unnamed—who have directly or indirectly contributed to my professional journey and to the development of this work.

This book is a reflection of collective learning, shared values, and a common commitment to delivering high-quality medicines for the benefit of patients worldwide.

-Author

Contents

CHAPTER 1

Introduction to Quality by Design

In pharma, **quality** means that a medicine is **safe, effective, pure, and consistent**, so that every dose a patient takes works as intended without causing harm. Like human race, pharmaceutical manufacturing and quality systems have evolved from primitive dispensing of powders to novel drug delivery systems and testing by organoleptic and gravimetric methods to advanced process analytical technology. The traditional pharmaceutical quality relied on end product testing for defined specifications to control quality and is called "Quality by Testing (QbT)". About 10-20 tablets are tested from a batch of 0.1 million to 1 million tablets to assure the quality of the entire batch, which is statistically inefficient to prove the results. In addition, the failure to meet specified quality attributes of end product lead to severe loss to the industry and re-processing of failed batches was also considered till they meet the desired specifications.

The reasons for failure of a batch to meet set specifications are unknown since the product development and manufacturing process were not investigated scientifically thoroughly to understand the effect of the material attributes, process variables and process controls on *quality* of finished product. Dr. Joseph M. Juran, a pioneer in quality management, introduced the term Quality by Design (QbD) in the 1980s. His philosophy is that *quality* should be planned and built into the product rather than testing the end product. The idea of "designing quality into products" originated outside pharmaceuticals, particularly in manufacturing and engineering industries.

In 1990s and early 2000, pharmaceutical industry has understood the significant of building quality into the product instead of testing the finished product. This shift is from Quality by Testing (QbT) to quality by design (QbD). Frequent failure of drug product quality, recalls from the market and unwanted side effects from drug products have been the focus of regulatory authorities across the globe. The USFDA has launched the initiative *"Pharmaceutical cGMPs for the 21st Century: A Risk-Based Approach"* in 2004, promoting science- and risk-based regulation. The Europe, Japan and other countries had series of meetings to address the quality issues and led to the formal incorporation of QbD into pharmaceutical regulations via the

International Council for Harmonisation (ICH). A series of ICH guidelines were issued from 2004.

- **ICH Q8 (2004, revised 2009):** *Pharmaceutical Development* – introduced QbD concepts like QTPP, CQAs, and design space.
- **ICH Q9 (2005):** *Quality Risk Management* – emphasized risk assessment tools.
- **ICH Q10 (2008):** *Pharmaceutical Quality System* – lifecycle approach to quality management
- **ICH Q11 (2012):** *Development and Manufacture of Drug Substances* – extended QbD principles to Active Pharmaceutical Ingredients (APIs).

"Quality by Design (QbD) is a systematic, science-based, and proactive approach to pharmaceutical development and manufacturing. It emphasizes that product quality should not be tested into the product at the end, but built into the product and process from the beginning" is the definition used.

Currently, QbD is not an option but the need to achieve high quality drug products development, scale up, manufacturing and continuous improvement. Pharmaceutical companies started applying QbD in:

- Formulation development (defining design space for excipients and processes).
- Analytical methods (Analytical QbD, or AQbD, for robust, reliable testing methods).
- Biologics and biosimilars, where complex processes require greater control.
- Continuous manufacturing and real-time release testing (RTRT).

Quality by Design (QbD) is not a process but it is a philosophy where the scientists apply their knowledge, literature, experimental data, statistical analysis, and risk assessment to understand the material attributes of excipients used, process parameters applied and their impact on quality attributes of product. The objective is to build the quality into the product and hence, the first step is to define the quality target product profile (QTPP). QTPP is nothing but list of specific characters of a dosage form that ensure safety, efficacy and quality. These QTPPs of finished product can be summarized into few Quality Attributes called Critical Quality Attributes (CQAs).

A drug product contains drug and excipients and they are subjected for processing to convert them into a suitable dosage form. For example, a drug, diluent, dry binder, glidant and lubricant are blended and compressed into an immediate release tablet. These materials have some attributes based on their functionality that would affect the tablets quality. For example, the surface area of lubricant is a critical character that affects the lubrication process and hence, the surface area of lubricant is called critical material attribute (CMA). One excipient may contain more than one CMA and all the materials critical attributes have to be identified so that systematic experimentation can be carried out to study their impact on CQAs. Apart from composition of formulation, the process used is also important for achieving desired quality. Pharmaceutical manufacturing comprises of several unit operations arranged in order. In direct compression example, blending of excipient, lubrication of blend in a blender followed by compression are the simple unit operations for the production of tablets.

The CMAs of drug and excipients are important for the blending and lubrication processes, and the output is the lubricated blend for compression. The lubricated blend characters such as assay of drug in blend, uniformity of drug in blend and blend flow properties are the CQAs of the lubricated blend. The blend CQAs are not only influenced by CMAs of materials used but also by the process parameters and hence, identification of critical process parameters (CPPs) of the blending operation is important so that proper control of CPPs can be used to produce blend with desired CQAs. It should be noted that the CQAs of lubricated blend are now CMAs to the next operation of tablet compression and the CPPs of compression process impact the CQAs of tablets.

Various QbD tools such as Ishikawa diagram or failure mode effect analysis (FMEA) are used for risk identification, risk analysis and risk management of quality. Risk identification is a systematic process to identify potential risks to product quality throughout the product lifecycle. Identified risks are now subjected for thorough analysis with respect to probability of occurrence, severity of harm and detectability of risk. Risk evaluations consider the strength of evidence for probability, severity, and detectability.

After identification of CMAs and CPPs, the next step is to carryout Pareto analysis of them to short list the most important CMAs and CPPs. Systematic study of impact of short-listed CMAs and CPPs on CQAs is carried out by the application of Design of Experiments (DoE). Design of Experiments (DOE) is a systematic and statistical approach for planning, conducting, and analysing controlled tests to understand how multiple input variables (factors) affect an output or response variable. Its core purpose is to determine which factors are most influential, optimize process settings, and achieve desired outcomes efficiently, saving time and resources compared to traditional one-factor-at-a-time experiments.

Design of experiments is carried out with the help of DoE software for screening the short-listed CMAs and CPPs that impact CQAs. The results from screening experiments are used to identify most impactful factors (CMA and CPP) on CQAs of the drug product. Optimization of these most influential factors is achieved using response surface methodology-based experiments such as full factorial designs, central composite design, mixture design, D-optimal etc. The results of these experiments are used to build mathematical models that relate the factors (CMAs and CPPs) and CQAs so that desired CQAs can be achieved using optimum factors. The experimental data allows the creation of design space for CMAs and CPPs within which the CQAs are met. A design space is defined as the multidimensional region of input variables (like process parameters and material attributes) that have been shown to consistently deliver a product meeting its quality requirements. Working within the established design space is considered normal process operation and is not a regulatory change, while operating outside it is a change that requires further review.

The measurement of CQAs can be in-line, on-line, at site or off-line. Measurement of specific characteristics of raw material, blend, or process parameter in-line or on-line using proper instruments enables continuous quality control, provides deep process understanding, optimizes processes for efficiency and cost-effectiveness. Process Analytical Technology (PAT) is used to design, analyse, and control manufacturing processes in real-time by measuring critical quality and performance attributes of raw materials and in-process materials to ensure final product quality. The data is inspected, transformed, and modelled using multivariate, artificial intelligence (AI) and machine learning methods to detect trends, predict outcomes, and enable immediate process adjustments or real-time release testing. Key goals include enhancing process understanding, improving operational efficiency, reducing reliance on offline testing, and ensuring product quality throughout the manufacturing lifecycle.

During the drug product development, the composition of a dosage form is finalized and the manufacturing process is optimized using the laboratory equipment. In general, the pharmaceutical composition is fixed and is *scale independent*. But the commercial production of drug product utilizes bigger equipment than those used in laboratory. Therefore, there is a need for systematic and scientific investigation to scale up the manufacturing process from laboratory scale to commercial scale. The CPPs are divided into scale independent and scale dependent. Scale independent process parameters are those process parameters that remain constant across the size of the batch. However, scale dependent parameters have to be optimized based on the commercial batch size using sound scientific principles and scale up techniques.

Once the scale up of the process at the commercial scale is established, there is a need to develop a control strategy to ensure batch to batch consistency in the quality of product. As per the USFDA a control strategy "is a planned set of controls, derived from an in-depth understanding of the product and process, designed to ensure process performance and product quality." Once the optimization of composition and process completes with design space, the controls for each critical process parameter are placed including CMAs. These controls would ensure the quality of drug product during the manufacturing of commercial batches.

All the QbD principles explained with the help of formulation development, process optimization and process validation are equally applicable to various analytical methods used to measure the attributes of raw materials, drug, packing material and finished product. The analytical method development, verification, optimization of critical method parameters (CMPs) and method validation should follow QbD principles including DoE. Creation of design space or method operable design region (MODR) for analytical method are highly useful for flexibility during regular analysis.

The drug product is supplied into the market upon receipt of marketing authorization from regulatory authorities by manufacturing the drug product at commercial scale regularly. The QbD frame work continues to measure the process capability and strives for continuous improvement in the quality of the product. The purpose of process capability is to provide statistical data on performance, identify areas of poor quality, set a baseline for improvement, and reduce defects and costs. The purpose of continuous improvement is to use this data and other feedback to constantly refine processes, eliminate waste, enhance quality, and boost efficiency and profitability over time.

Quality by Design is a philosophy that focus on building quality to into the product by studying the impact of variables with most advanced scientific principles on critical quality attributes, creating design space, monitoring process capability and engaging in continuous improvement in quality of the product. Quality should be built into the product but not test for. QbD is a journey throughout the life cycle of the product not a destiny.

CHAPTER 2

Elements of Quality by Design

The important elements of quality by design (QbD) are discussed in this chapter. First of all, a quality target product profile (QTPP) is defined that contain desired quality features of a drug product keeping in mind the safety and efficacy of the product and patient compliance. The other elements of QbD are to achieve the QTPP.

2.1 Quality Target Product Profile (QTPP)

It is a document prepared before the initiation of drug product development. It summarises the ideal quality characters of a drug product to ensure the desired quality, safety and efficacy of drug product based on intended use and regulatory requirements **Table 2.1**.

In case of generic product development, much of the information is obtained from the innovator product characteristics. The important components of QTPP are based on active ingredient, excipients, dosage form and packaging. QTPP is based on dosage form, clinical use and quality of finished product. The following table shows the elements of QTPP for an immediate release tablet having 80mg of API.

Table 2.1 Quality Target Product Profile (QTPP) of an immediate release oral tablet.

Profile component	Target	Justification/Reference
Dosage Form	Tablet	Generic Product needs to be same as that of Reference Product; Pharmaceutical equivalence requirement: same dosage form; Ref: Reference Product PIL
Dosage design	Immediate release tablet	Immediate release design need to meet label claims
Route of administration	Oral	Pharmaceutical equivalence requirement: same route of administration

Table 2.1: *Contd...*

Profile component	Target	Justification/Reference
Dosage strength	40 mg and 80 mg	Pharmaceutical equivalence requirement: same strength
Therapeutic class	Androgen receptor inhibitor	Same as Reference (Reference Product)
Maximum daily dose	160 mg	As per reference product PIL
Therapeutic use	Used for the treatment of: Castration-resistant prostate cancer and metastatic castration-sensitive prostate cancer.	Same as Reference (Reference Product)
Drug product quality attributes (Physical & Chemical)	Physical attributes (Hardness, Disintegration test etc.)	Pharmaceutical equivalence requirement: Must meet the same compendial or other applicable (quality) standards (i.e., identity, assay, purity, and quality).
	Identification	
	Assay	
	Content Uniformity	
	Dissolution	
	Degradation products	
	Residual Solvents	
	Water content	
	Microbial Limits	
Storage condition	20°C to 25°C (68°F to 77°F) in a dry place and keep the container tightly closed. Excursions permitted from 15°C to 30°C (59°F to 86°F)	As per the reference product PIL
Photo stability	Should comply to product shelf life specification for related substances	As per ICH Q1b
Stability	Product should be stable for at least 24-Months at room temperature	Drug product stability is required to establish shelf life of drug product.
Bioequivalence	Should be bioequivalent to reference drug product.	Generic formulation should be bioequivalent to that of reference drug product.
Container and Closure system	**40 mg:** Bottles of 120 tablets with child resistant closures (NDC 0469-0625-99) **80 mg:** Bottles of 60 tablets with child resistant closures (NDC 0469-0725-60)	The suitable pack similar to the Reference product /based on stability studies to be finalized

Type of dosage form, dosage form design, strength(s) and route of administration are related to dosage form while therapeutic class, therapeutic use and maximum daily dose are related to clinical usage, and product quality attributes, container & closure system, stability, and bioequivalence are related to drug product performance.

QTPP for injections, topical preparations, respiratory products etc., have to be defined individually based on the expected performance of the drug product. Sterility and osmolality and other characters may be important while viscosity, spreadability, packaging and applicator etc., are considered.

2.2 Critical Quality Attributes (CQAs)

Critical Quality Attributes (CQAs) are physical, chemical, biological, or microbiological properties or characteristics of a pharmaceutical product that must be controlled within defined limits to ensure the desired product quality, safety, and efficacy **Table 2.2**. The CQAs of the finished product are defined so that the QTPP is achieved. Hence, CQAs have to be monitored during the product development. Not all desired characters of the product are critical since one CQA may also ensure more than one character. For example, dissolution may be a surrogate for disintegration of a tablet and hence, monitoring dissolution of tablet may be sufficient.

CQAs are not only important for finished product but also for intermediate stages. For example, a tablet manufactured by direct compression has process steps of weighing, sieving, blending and compression. Now the lubricated blend CQAs are blend uniformity and blend assay which intern impact the CQAs of finished product. Hence, when a battery of unit operations is involved, it is advisable to define CQAs for each output so that quality of finished product is ensured. In case of wet granulation process, steps of weighing, sieving, granulation, drying, milling, sieving, blending and compression are involved. The output of one-unit operation serves as an input to the next unit operation.

The following table shows all quality attributes but identifies the CQAs of an immediate release tablet whose QTPP is defined above.

Table 2.2 Critical Quality Attributes (CQAs) of Immediate Release Tablet.

Quality attributes of the drug product (Physical & Chemical)		Target	Is this a CQA	Justification
Physical Attributes	Appearance	**40 mg:** Yellow, round, film-coated tablets debossed with E 40 **80 mg:** Yellow, oval, film-coated tablets debossed with E 80	No	Colour, shape and appearance are not directly linked to safety and efficacy. Therefore, they are not critical. The target is to achieve similarity to reference product.
Physical Attributes	Odour	No Characteristic odour	No	In general, a noticeable odour is not directly linked to safety and efficacy.
Physical Attributes	Size	Similar to Reference Product	No	For comparable ease of swallowing as well as acceptance and compliance with treatment regimens, the target for tablet dimensions is set similar to the RLD.
Physical Attributes	Score Configuration	No Break-line	No	No break-line means the tablet should not be broken and should be used whole.
Physical Attributes	Friability	NMT 1.0% w/w	No	A target of NMT 1.0% w/w of mean weight loss assures a low impact on safety and efficacy and minimizes customer complaints.
Hardness		Sufficient to have Friability <1.0%w/w.	No	Hardness can have impact on the dissolution. However, it will be controlled during compression.
Identification Test 1		The retention time of the major peak of the Sample solution corresponds to the peak of the Standard solution as obtained in the Assay.	Yes*	Formulation and process variables do not impact identity. Therefore, this CQA will not be monitored during formulation and process development

Table 2.2 *Contd...*

Quality attributes of the drug product (Physical & Chemical)	Target	Is this a CQA	Justification
Identification Test 2	The spectrum of the test specimen of the Enzalutamide should be concordant with the respective standard.	Yes*	
Disintegration	Should disintegrate within 15 min	Yes	Disintegration of tablets impacts the dissolution rate and extent. Hence, it is assessed throughout the product development.
Dissolution	Drug release NLT 80.0% in 45 minutes. Shall be revised based on data of RLD and Test product.	Yes	Failure to meet the dissolution specification can impact bioavailability. Both formulation and process variables affect the dissolution profile. This CQA will be investigated throughout the formulation and process development.
Water content	Less than 5%w/w	Yes	High water content may affect the degradation and microbial growth of the drug product and can be a potential CQA.
Assay	Each Tablet contains- not less than 95.0% and not more than 105.0% of labelled amount of drug.	Yes	Assay variability will affect safety and efficacy. Thus, the assay will be evaluated throughout product and process development.
Uniformity of Dosage Units	Conforms to USP<905>Uniformity of Dosage Units	Yes	Variability in content uniformity will affect safety and efficacy. Both formulation and process variables impact content uniformity, so this CQA will be evaluated throughout product and process development.

Table 2.2 *Contd...*

Quality attributes of the drug product (Physical & Chemical)	Target	Is this a CQA	Justification
Related substances	As per ICH Q3A, Q3B, Q3C & Q3D	Yes	Degradation products can impact safety and must be controlled based on compendial/ICH requirements or Reference product characterization to limit patient exposure. The target for any unknown impurity is set according to the ICH identification threshold for this drug product. Formulation and process variables can impact degradation products. Therefore, degradation products will be assessed during product and process development.
Residual solvents	USP <467>option 1	Yes*	Residual solvents can impact safety. However, no solvent is used in the drug product manufacturing process and the drug product complies with USP Option 1. Therefore, formulation and process variables are unlikely to impact this CQA.
Microbial Limits	To be established	Yes*	Non-compliance with microbial limits will impact patient safety.

*These CQAs are not monitored continuously during drug product development but ensured to be within acceptable limits.

The CQAs vary for each product based on its QTPP. The product CQAs are monitored for all important batches manufactured during the development. The formulation composition and process changes are used to manufacture drug product and the CQAs are assessed to select best batches that meet defined limits of all CQAs.

2.3 Critical Material Attributes (CMAs)

CMAs are specific, measurable properties of input materials that can significantly influence the quality of a final product. Three main components of a drug product are active pharmaceutical Ingredient (API), excipients and primary packing materials. Solvents or some material are used during the manufacturing of the product but they are not present in the finished product. The critical material attributes of these materials are also important in some cases.

(a) *Active Pharmaceutical Ingredient (API)*

The chemical substance responsible for observed clinical benefit is called API. The physical, chemical, microbiological and other properties of API that are critical for product quality, safety and efficacy are called CMAs of API.

Physical Properties

The following physical properties of API are considered for identifying the critical material attributes for the finished product. Each property has to be evaluated based on the dosage form, strength, drug release mechanism, manufacturing and stability.

(a) Polymorphism
(b) Particle shape
(c) Particle size and distribution
(d) Porosity
(e) Bulk density, tapped density and flow properties
(f) Compressibility
(g) Hygroscopicity

(a) *Polymorphism*: Polymorphs of an API exhibit different solubility, dissolution and stability characters. Therefore, a thorough review of the polymorphic forms and their characters is required to identify the criticality of this material property. In generic product development, use of polymorphic form other than the one used in innovator product may be warranted due to patents. In such case, this property becomes a critical material attribute and its monitoring is required during development and on stability.

(b) *Particle shape*: Different shapes of drug particles can affect flowability, dissolution rate, and bioavailability. The drug distribution during blending and compressibility are also affected by particle shape. Hence, the significance of this property in the drug product has to be assessed.

(c) *Particle size and distribution*: The average particle size and also the particle size distribution influence the dissolution rate especially for poorly soluble drugs and drug distribution in the blend most importantly when the drug dose is low.

(d) *Porosity*: Porosity refers to the pores present in the particle of drug. Higher porosity increases the fluid penetration into the particle and increases the dissolution rate of drug due to higher surface area leading to improved bioavailability.

(e) *Bulk density, tapped density and flow properties*: These properties are more relevant to powders, capsules and tablets where the flow of the final blend is critical for high speed operations. The compressibility depends on bulk density and tapped density which is required to form a solid compact.

(f) *Compressibility*: The Compressibility Index, also known as Carr's index is a measure of a powder's ability to be compressed, reflecting its flow properties. It is calculated using bulk and tapped densities, with lower values indicating better flowability.

(g) *Hygroscopicity*: The ability of API to take up moisture from the environment and hold is called hygroscopicity. The water taken from air can be by adsorption where the water molecules are on the surface of drug particle or by absorption where the water molecules penetrate into the inner part of drug particle. Hygroscopicity increases the water content of the API and leads degradation and microbial growth in the drug product. The humidity and temperature of the air influences the water absorption by API. It may be necessary to manufacture the dosage form in low humidity and temperature conditions.

Chemical Properties

1. Solubility
2. Intrinsic Dissolution
3. Stability
4. Impurities or Related Substances (RS)

1. *Solubility*: Solubility of API in water, aqueous buffers and organic solvents is important since processing of API during dosage form manufacturing needs drug in solution form in some cases. In addition, drug solubility affects dissolution and bioavailability.
2. *Intrinsic Dissolution*: Intrinsic dissolution of API is a measure of how quickly API goes into solution under controlled conditions. It specifically focuses on the dissolution rate of a compound while maintaining a constant surface area, temperature, pH, and other relevant factors. Intrinsic dissolution of API is an important property

in the selection of specific polymorph, particle size, particle size distribution and specific surface area of an API.

3. *Stability*: This material attribute directly impacts the quality, safety and efficacy of the drug product. Physical and/or chemical instability of API would significantly affect the drug product.
4. *Impurities or Related Substances*: API may contain organic or inorganic compounds unrelated to drug chemical structure that have been used during the manufacture of API. The related substances are those compounds that are structurally similar to API but differ in functional groups arising from intermediates used in the manufacture or formed due to degradation of API.

Others

A. Water content

B. Residual Solvents

C. Elemental impurities

D. Nitrosamines and genotoxic impurities

A. *Water Content*: The water presents in the API in bound form and/or unbound form. If the water molecule is part of the crystal structure of API, called hydrates, this water is called bound water. Water molecules present freely in API are unbound water. The unbound water varies based on external conditions and on storage while bound water is constant. The unbound water content is critical since it supports degradation and microbial growth in the finished product.

B. *Residual Solvents*: Various solvents are used during the synthesis of API and some synthetic process involves several steps. The solvents used in the synthesis are removed carefully but some quantity of solvent remains in the API called residual solvent. Most of the residual organic solvents are hazardous to health. Hence, the levels of these solvents have to be controlled within the permissible limits.

C. *Elemental Impurities*: These impurities, which are inorganic in nature, can originate from various sources during the manufacturing process and can be toxic even at low levels.

D. *Nitrosamines and genotoxic impurities*: *Nitrosamine impurities, even in trace amounts, are highly toxic* and mutagenic, capable of damaging DNA, and subsequently increase the risk of cancer incidence. Genotoxic impurities due to their potential to cause deleterious changes in the genetic material of cells, even at very low levels are to be avoided or minimized to very low levels. This can lead to mutations and potentially cause cancer, posing a significant risk to patient safety.

It should be noted that all the CMAs listed above are not considered for every API but each material property is considered, reviewed and then its inclusion or exclusion is decided. For example, a drug does not exhibit polymorphism then there is no need include polymorphism as a CMA. If a drug has no nitrogen atom in its structure, need not be considered for nitrosamine impurities and particle size may not be a CMA for a highly water-soluble drug. Most of the times many of the CMAs are controlled within the limits before using the API in the formulation development and only those CMAs that are important for the drug product are considered.

After the identification of CMAs of the API by prior knowledge, many of the CMAs are controlled by the API manufacturer while some CMAs are evaluated during product development to fix the limits. These CMAs are monitored through specifications of API so that the input quality of API is always within the acceptable limits. The CMAs are categorized into green (Low risk is acceptable), yellow (medium risk but to be understood during product development) and red (risk is high and hence, to be monitored throughout the development and during manufacturing) **Table 2.3**.

Table 2.3 Critical Material Attributes of API.

Drug Product CQA's	Drug Substance Attributes						
	Particle size distribution	Hygrosco-picity	Solubility	Water Content	Residual solvents	Flow properties	Solid State Form
Assay	Low	Low	Low	Low	Low	Low	Low
Uniformity of dosage units	Low	Low	Low	Low	Low	Low	Low
Dissolution	Low	Low	medium	Low	Low	Low	High
Related substance	Low	Low	Low	Low	Low	Low	Low

	Low risk- Acceptable	No further investigation
	Medium risk	To be reviewed during development
	High risk	To be studied experimentally

(b) *Excipients*

Excipients are selected to impart specific functions to the finished dosage form and many types of excipients are required for manufacturing a dosage form. Excipients do have material attributes that are critical for the quality of the product. Each excipient selection involves both qualitative grade and quantity to be used in the formulation. The general excipients used in immediate release tablet manufactured by wet granulation are diluent, binder, disinstegrant, glidant and lubricant. However, colours, flavours and sweeteners are used for organoleptic properties and for patient compliance. Diluents are mainly used to increase tablet size so as to accommodate low dose drug into usable form. In addition, they are also used to improve flow of blend and compressibility. Therefore, the critical material attributes of excipients have to be listed, reviewed, then some CMAs have to be controlled during manufacturing of excipients while other CMAs are evaluated experimentally during the drug product development to define the limits of those CMAs.

In generic product development, qualitative composition is arrived at by understanding innovator product composition, prior knowledge, and desired functionality of excipient. All the excipients are now subjected for evaluation of their critical material attributes (CMAs).

The CMAs of a particular excipient are now listed and risk analysis is done to categorise the CMAs into low, medium and high risk. For example, the CMAs of Microcrystalline cellulose are particle size and distribution, moisture content, tapped density, and pH **Table 2.4**.

Table 2.4 Critical Material Attributes of Microcrystalline Cellulose.

Drug Product CQAs	**Microcrystalline Cellulose**				
	PSD	**Tapped density**	**Moisture content**	**pH**	**Quantity**
Assay	Low	Low	Low	Low	Medium
UOD	Medium	Low	Low	Low	Medium
Dissolution	Low	Medium	Low	Low	Medium
Related substances	Low	Low	High	Medium	Low

CMAs influence on the CQAs of finished product are listed in the **Table 2.4.** The categorization of CMA into low, medium and high is based on the drug and dosage form. The justification for categorizing impact of CMA on a particular CQA of the product has to be documented. In this case, drug is sensitive to moisture and hence, the risk is high if the moisture content of MCC is high. The PSD of MCC and its quantity impact the low dose drug distribution in the blend during dry mixing before wet granulation and hence, medium risk is anticipated for unit of dose (UOD).

Similar exercise has to be made for all the excipients to document the expected quality risk from CMAs of excipients and based on the categorization, a summary table that provides high level view of excipients and impact on CQAs. **Table 2.5** shows the summary of effect of excipients on CQAs of product.

Table 2.5 Effect of Excipients on CQAs of drug product.

Drug Product CQAs	**Excipients**				
	Diluent	**Binder**	**Disintegrant**	**Glidant**	**Lubricant**
Assay	Low	Low	Low	Low	Low
UOD	Medium	Low	Low	Low	Low
Dissolution	Medium	Medium	Medium	Low	Low
Related substances	High	Low	Low	Low	Low

Table 2.5 summary provides the path to conduct experiments and gain knowledge on the impact of excipient on CQAs of drug product. Conducting experiments with different PSDs of MCC keeping all other excipients constant would provide UOD data to conclude the effect of PSD of MCC and define the desired PSD specification.

(c) *Container and Closure System*

Different dosage forms require different containers and closures. Tablets and capsules are packed in bottles and/or blisters. Critical Material Attributes (CMAs) for bottle packaging are the key properties of the bottle material and design that directly impact the quality and performance of the packaged product. Polyethylene terephthalate (PET), High density polyethylene (HDPE) and glass bottles (transparent and amber colour or any other colour) are used in packing the tablets or capsules. The critical material attributes (CMAs) of Packing material have to be reviewed critically and the impact of CMAs on the quality, safety and efficacy of the product have to be assessed. In this example, HDPE bottle is selected as primary packing material with child resistance cap **Table 2.6**.

Table 2.6 Effect of CMAs of HDPE bottle with CR cap on CQAs of product.

Drug Product CQAs	HDPE Bottle with CR cap				
	Chemical resistance	**Size**	**Moisture permeation**	**Flexibility**	**CR cap**
Assay	Low	Low	Low	Low	Low
UOD	Low	Low	Low	Low	Low
Dissolution	Low	Low	Low	Low	Low
Related substances	Low	Medium	Medium	Low	Low

HDPE bottles offer many advantages and child resistant cap is to prevent accidental consumption of drug by children. The drug is sensitive to moisture and hence, the head space in the bottle and moisture permeation rate under different humidity and temperature conditions influence the degradation of drug. Hence, medium risk is anticipated since the head space is minimised by selecting suitable size and high-density polyethylene has low moisture permeation. However, the Related Substances are monitored by conducting experiments under different humidity and temperature conditions to address this issue during development.

(d) *Other components used in drug product manufacturing*

Sometimes solvents such as ethanol, isopropyl alcohol, etc., are used in the manufacture of tablets but these solvents are removed from the dosage form. Isopropyl alcohol (IPA) is used in the wet granulation of the drug in this example since the drug is sensitive to the water. Even though IPA is not present in the finished product in significant amounts, the CMAs of IPA influence the CQAs of product and the manufacturing process. Hence, the CMAs of IPA are listed, reviewed and risk analysis is carried out to assess the impact on CQAs of product.

The CMAs of IPA include purity, solvent power, flammability, toxicity and odour. IPA is a hygroscopic solvent and hence, absorbs water from air and the purity is reduced. Solubility of binder in IPA is important since high concentration of binder is used in wet granulation. Odour and toxicity may not be an issue if the levels of IPA in finished product are well below the permitted level of 0.5%. IPA is a flammable solvent with low flash point and hence, the equipment used should be flame proof and care has to be taken during wet granulation and drying.

2.4 Critical Process Parameters (CPP)

Critical Process Parameters (CPPs) are key process variables that significantly impact the quality of a product in pharmaceutical manufacturing. Pharmaceutical manufacturing is currently a batch process in which a series of unit operations are involved. Efforts are in place for continuous manufacturing and some companies have established continuous manufacturing where unit operations are carried out continuously.

The CMAs of raw materials used in the formulation are critical since the output material from first unit operation is the feed for next unit operations. The manufacturing immediate release tablet by batch process is considered to describe the critical process parameters of a unit operation. The flow of the unit operations in manufacturing of immediate release tablet is given below.

1. Weighing of API and excipients	2. Shifting of materials	3. Dry mixing of materials in a blender	4. Wet granulation in (RMG)	5. Drying in Fluid Bed Drier
6. Milling using a co-mill/ Multi-mill	7. Shifting with specific mesh size to obtain granules	8. Blending of granules with extra-granular materials	9. Lubrication of Blend with lubricant	10. Compression on tablet machine

Unit operation 3, dry mixing of materials in a blender, is performed to get uniform distribution of API and all the materials. The mixed blend is now loaded into the RMG and binder solution is added and wet granule mass is loaded into FBD for drying and so on. The unit process is generally depicted as given below.

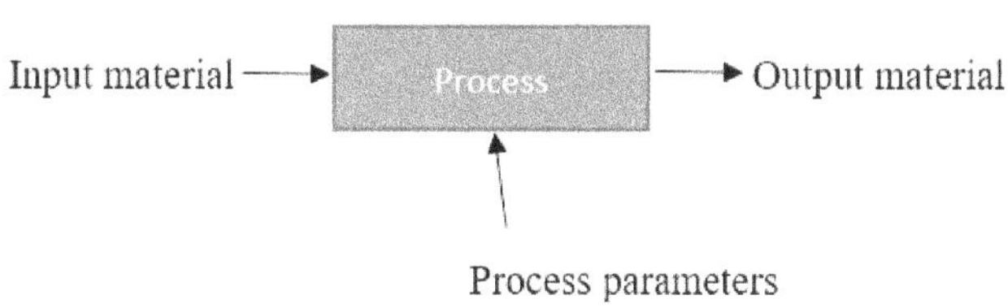

Input material CMAs are fixed and output material CQAs are defined. Now, the process parameters have to be determined for obtaining desired CQAs of output material with the input materials. The dry mixing process parameters are order of addition of materials, blender type & size, occupancy of blender (percent of volume occupied by the materials), blender rotational speed and duration of mixing. Usually blender type & size and order of addition of materials are fixed and then the remaining process parameters are percent occupancy, rpm of blender and duration of mixing. These process parameters influence the uniform distribution of API and hence, experiments are conducted to fix the operational range of these parameters called Critical Process Parameters (CPPs) either by one factor at time (OFAT) or design of experiments (DoE).

It should be noted that the output materials (called intermediates) from one-unit operation are input materials for next unit operation and hence, the CQAs of output material of earlier operation become CMAs for next unit operation. The CPPs of each unit operation have to be optimized for achieving desired quality and the range of each CPP is defined **Table 2.7**.

Each unit operation CPPs are listed, thoroughly reviewed and risk analysis is carried out to identify the impact of each unit operation on CQAs of drug product.

Table 2.7 Effect of unit operations on CQAs of drug product.

CQA's of Drug Product	Unit Operation						
	Dry Blending	**RMG Granulation**	**Drying**	**Milling**	**Sieving**	**Blending & Lubrication**	**Compression**
Assay	Low	Low	Low	Low	Low	Low	Low
Uniformity of Dosage units	Medium	Low	Low	Low	Low	Medium	Low
Dissolution	Low	High	Low	Medium	Low	Medium	Medium
Related substances	Low	Low	Medium	Low	Low	Low	Low

The categorization of quality risk as low, medium and high has to be justified scientifically after thorough debate by cross functional team. This step is critical since the subsequent experimental design and collection of data depends on this judgement. For example, the following table shows the categorization of risk from dry blending operation on the CQAs of drug product and offers the scientific justification **Table 2.7(a)**.

Table 2.7(a) Scientific justification of categorization of risk for CQAs of drug product by Dry Blending operation

Drug Product CQAs	Risk	Scientific Justification
Assay	Low	The overall blend assay after dry blending is expected to be within the limits
UOD	Medium	The blend uniformity at the unit dose level may vary leading to failure of UOD
Dissolution	Low	This operation has no impact on dissolution
Related Substances	Low	This operation has no impact on Related Substances

This type of table showing the justification for risk assessment has to be prepared for each unit operation involved in the manufacture of dosage form to arrive at overall impact of each operation on the CQAs of drug product.

The CPPs are classified into scale independent and scale dependent. Scale independent CPPs can be optimized at any scale but scale dependent CPPs have to be optimized at the commercial scale. Therefore, it is necessary to list both class of CPPs for each unit operation. For example, the scale independent and dependent CPPs of blending unit operation are given in **Table 2.8** assuming that same type of blender is used in higher scale also.

Table 2.8 Scale dependent and Independent CPPs of Blending operation.

CPP	Scale Dependent/ Independent
RPM	Dependent
Time of operation	Dependent
Occupancy	Independent
Tip speed	Independent

Tip speed = π*D*RPM where D is the diameter of the Blender and RPM is rotations per minute.

Similarly, the scale dependent and independent parameters of RMG granulation can be listed **Table 2.9**. The scale dependent parameters can be optimized during product development at the lab scale and scale dependent parameters are optimized at the desired scale using engineering principles.

Table 2.9 Scale dependent and Independent CPPs of Granulation (RMG).

CPP	Scale Dependent/ Independent
Impeller speed & Chopper speed	Dependent
Binder addition time	Dependent
Binder solution volume	Dependent
Kneading time	Dependent
Occupancy	Independent
Tip speed of impeller	Independent

The CPPs of all unit operations are optimized to get desired CQAs of output materials (intermediates) and finally finished product. Once the CPPs for each unit operation are optimized, then operational range of the CPPs are fixed that produce constant quality of finished product.

2.5 Design Space

Design Space (DS) is defined as the multidimensional combination and interaction of input variables (e.g., material attributes) and process parameters that have been demonstrated to provide assurance of quality.

Critical material attributes of each raw material are identified and the range of the values for each CMA are defined that would be controlled as specification. For example, Particle size distribution (PSD) is identified as a CMA for a poorly soluble API. A three-tier specification is defined for PSD of API as D90 < 20um, D50 < 10um and D10 < 4um based on experiments conducted with different PSD of API. Similarly, specification for each CMA of API is defined so that input API meets specification for all CMA. This ensures constant input of API into the manufacturing process. This process of defining specification for CMA of each excipient is carried out so that all the quality of materials used in the manufacturing of drug product are controlled via specifications. In general, excipient vendors offer certain grades of excipients with defined CMAs and range of values. Hence, a formulation scientist selects suitable grade based on prior knowledge and experimental data generated using different grades of excipients. In other words, formulation scientist has the flexibility of selecting a grade of excipient from a particular vendor whose CMAs are controlled by the excipient manufacturer.

Once the qualitative and quantitative composition of drug product is finalized, the process parameters of a unit operation that influence the CQAs of the drug product have to be studies to fix the operational range within which the quality of drug product is maintained. Since, the pharmaceutical manufacturing is a batch process, creation of design space for each unit operation is preferred rather than for entire chain of unit operations involved.

The first unit operation of the manufacturing process gets raw materials as input variables and the process variables produce output material (intermediate) with varied CQAs. Therefore, the CQAs of intermediate have to defined with acceptable range. For example, the dry blending in the immediate release tablet receives initial raw materials and processed by blender with varied process variables such as occupancy, speed, and duration of blending. The resultant blend is analysed for its CQAs such as blend assay and blend uniformity. The acceptance criteria for blend assay is 97-103% of drug and for blend uniformity (determined by analysing 10 samples collected at 10 different locations in blender) is 90-110% of drug. Experiments are conducted for 3 variables (occupancy, speed and duration of blending) at two levels for each variable would give 8 experiments. The blend assay and blend uniformity data is generated for each experiment to verify whether the CQAs are met or not. The data is analysed statistically using a software program to identify the operational range of process variables. This process allows the fixation of process parameters range that would always provide desired CQAs (Blend assay and Blend uniformity in this case).

Another example is the determination of design space for hardness of tablets and the CQAs are Friability of <1.0%w/w and dissolution >80% at 15 minutes. Tablets are compressed at various hardness levels (2 to 16kp), and friability and drug release at 15 minutes are determined for the tablets. **Table 2.10** shows the data obtained in the experiments.

Table 2.10 Effect of hardness on friability and dissolution of tablet.

Hardness (kp)	**Friability %w/w**	**Dissolution at 15 minutes**
2	1.5	**95**
4	1.3	**90**
6	1.3	**88**
8	**0.9**	**86**
10	**0.8**	**85**
12	**0.6**	**84**
14	**0.3**	78
16	**0.1**	70

Two CQAs have to be in acceptable limits for a given hardness. The hardness from 8 to 16kp is meeting friability criteria whereas hardness from 2 to 12kp is meeting dissolution criteria. The design space for both the CQAs lies from 8 to 12kp. It means the hardness in this range meets both friability and dissolution criteria.

2.6 Control Strategy

Control strategy is a planned set of controls, derived from a deep understanding of the product and its process, that ensures process performance and product quality. The control strategy includes drug substance, excipients, packaging material, facilities, equipment, process parameters, in-process controls, and finished product specifications.

Planned Controls

Deep understanding of CMAs, CPPs, intermediate CQAs and finished product CQAs is essential in finalizing the controls. API and excipients CMAs are controlled through specifications, intermediate CQAs are defined and determined during the development and manufacturing, and finally the quality of finished product is controlled through specifications.

Proactive and Reactive Controls

Proactive controls in Quality by Design (QbD) are preventative measures implemented throughout the product lifecycle to ensure consistent quality and minimize the risk of deviations from desired product characteristics. These controls are established during the design phase and focus on understanding and managing potential sources of variability in the manufacturing process. By proactively addressing these factors, QbD aims to build quality into the product from the outset, rather than relying solely on end-product testing.

Reactive Controls

Reactive controls are measures taken to detect and correct deviations from the established design space after they have occurred. These controls are part of the overall control strategy designed to ensure consistent product quality and process performance.

Monitoring and Feedback

Continuous monitoring of critical quality attributes (CQAs) and process parameters, coupled with timely feedback mechanisms, enables real-time adjustments and iterative improvements throughout the manufacturing process. For example, monitoring of granulation process by continuously measuring the power consumption and comparing it to the normal values would help to get desired output from RMG. Feedback mechanism is to use the data and adjust the process parameters of the downstream operation. For example, The PSD of the blend is slightly higher than normal range, then downstream unit operation, blending process parameters are adjusted to get blend uniformity and blend assay provided that the CPPs are within the operational range or within the design space.

Evolutionary Nature

The control strategy is not a static document but is continuously modified based on the knowledge gained during the manufacturing of the product and gathering the information from monitoring, change control and feedback information.

2.7 Continuous Improvement

Continuous improvement in the process is the key aspect of QbD. The knowledge accumulated during the manufacturing of commercial batches is gathered, organized and analysed to get insights into the CPPs and quality of the product. Efforts are made to improve the understanding of CPPs and the design space of proven operational ranges are continuously improved to manufacture quality product.

CHAPTER 3

Quality Risk Management

At the beginning of product development, QTPP is defined and then the possible risks are identified, evaluated and mitigation plans are made to eliminate or at least reduce the risks to acceptable level. The main principle of QbD is to build quality into the product not testing of finished product. The risk management refers to the efforts made to continuously reduce the risk by implementing proper mitigation plans during development and manufacturing. This proactive approach helps ensure product safety, efficacy, and consistent quality throughout the product lifecycle.

It should be noted that the safety and efficacy of drug product is established with clinical batches used in the studies. The Critical Quality Attributes (CQAs) of the clinical batches are the guiding principles that have to be maintained throughout the life cycle of the drug product. Hence, while safety and efficacy are established only once but the quality of the product has to be monitored throughout the life cycle of the drug product using QRM and Pharmaceutical Quality System (PQS).

The key stake holders of drug product quality are pharmaceutical industry, doctors, regulatory authorities and patients. The first three stake holders are for patients since the patient is the end user of the product and product quality risk directly effects the patients. Therefore, every risk assessment should consider the patient and QRM should ensure highest quality of the product.

ICH Q9 guidelines provides the details of Quality Risk Management (QRM). The step by step process is outlined in **Figure 3.1.** Risk assessment, risk control, risk review, risk communication and risk management tools are the key elements of QRM.

A person or team is designated as the process owner for QRM in the pharmaceutical industry. They have to lay down the process for QRM, the representatives from different departments have to be trained on QRM policy and process, and the decisions have to be implemented effectively across the company. All the necessary facilities, resources and finance have to be provided for effective implementation of QRM.

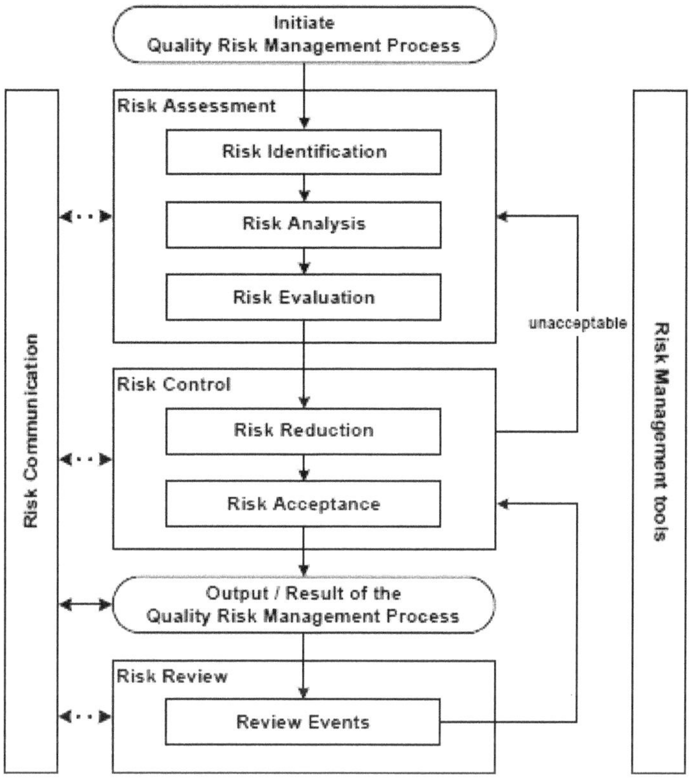

Figure 3.1 Quality Risk Management Process.

3.1 Risk Assessment

Quality Risk Assessment (QRA) within QbD is a systematic process used to identify, analyse, and evaluate potential risks to product quality throughout the drug development and manufacturing lifecycle. Multi-functional team members constitute a risk assessment team. At least one member from business development, formulation development, analytical development, technology transfer, bioequivalence and clinical, manufacturing, quality control and quality assurance teams are included in risk assessment team. It helps prioritize efforts, focus resources, and establish control strategies to ensure product quality, patient safety, and regulatory compliance.

Risk assessment consists of risk identification, risk analysis and risk evaluation. The *risk* is defined as the combination of the probability of occurrence of *harm* and the *severity* of that harm due lack of desired quality of drug product.

Risk Identification

Risk identification is a systematic process to identify potential risks to product quality throughout the product lifecycle. Drug product development starts with the selection of qualitative and quantitative composition based on prior knowledge, innovator composition in case of generic product, physicochemical properties of API and excipients, intended dosage form, route of administration and strength. A tentative process is selected for the manufacture of the dosage form and each unit operation involved is listed as a flow chart. The tentative analytical methods for CQAs are proposed. Now the team of experts in different fields are assembled in the meeting room under the leadership of QRM leader.

The risk identification is carried out taking the CMAs and CPPs of each unit operation into consideration. The basic question is "What might go wrong?". If something is expected to go wrong, then what are the consequences? This step identifies the problem or risk to the quality. There will be a list of risks identified by brain storming in this process. The assumptions made, the scientific basis for the assumptions, or prior knowledge or any other data has to be documented for each identified risk.

Risk Analysis

Identified risks are now subjected for thorough analysis with respect to probability of occurrence, severity of harm and detectability of risk. Probability refers to the occurrence of risk per a given number of events and can be expressed as percent. For example, the probability is 1% means, the risk may occur one in hundred times of the operation. Severity refers to the potential impact of a failure mode on product quality, patient safety, or regulatory compliance. The severity can be minor, moderate or severe to the patient. Detectability is the ability to identify a potential failure or deviation before it impacts product quality or well before the product is released for distribution into the market so that patient is protected. High detectability means a problem can be caught early, allowing for timely corrective action and minimizing negative consequences.

Risk Evaluation

It compares the identified and analysed risk against given risk criteria. Risk evaluations consider the strength of evidence for probability, severity, and detectability. The uncertainty of the risk assessment comes from incomplete knowledge on product composition and process variability (known or unknown). Typical sources of uncertainty include gaps in knowledge in pharmaceutical science and process understanding, sources of harm (e.g., failure modes of a process, sources of variability), and probability of detection of problems.

The output of risk assessment provides either a qualitative measure such as low, medium or high or a quantitative measure in numerical values. It is always advisable to convert the final risk assessment into numbers so that different risks can be compared. For example, 1 for low, 3 for medium and 5 for high. Some risk management tools use a relative risk measure to combine multiple levels of severity and probability into an overall estimate of relative risk.

3.2 Risk Control

The first step after completing the risk assessment is to decide whether the risk is acceptable or need to be controlled. This is a critical step since decision to reduce the risk or not is going to dictate the need for additional experiments, resources and finance. Therefore, a thorough review of the risk assessment and use of quality risk management tools for taking appropriate decision is important. How to reduce the risk? What tools and techniques are available for risk reduction? What is the appropriate balance among benefits, risks and resources? Are new risks introduced as a result of the identified risks being controlled? All these questions have to be addressed before initiating the control measure.

Risk Reduction

Risk reduction focuses on processes for mitigation or avoidance of quality risk when it exceeds a specified (acceptable) level. This includes implementing stronger process controls, optimizing process parameters, and developing robust analytical methods. All these processes are to reduce occurrence, severity, and improve detectability of the identified risk.

Reducing the *probability of risk* involves identifying potential failure modes, assessing their likelihood, and implementing preventative and detective controls to minimize the chance of their occurrence.

Risk *Severity* is the expected harm or adverse effect that may occur due to exposure to the Risk. In other words, it measures how bad things could get if a particular Risk materializes. When the Risk Severity is high, it means that the potential harm is also high, and, as a result, more attention and resources should be devoted to managing that Risk. Conversely, when the Risk Severity is low, the potential harm is also considered low, and less attention may be needed to manage it.

Detectability is the ability to identify a potential failure or deviation before it impacts product quality. Therefore, the detection methods are placed upstream of the unit operations and also at various intermediate CQAs so that the risk is detected early and appropriate changes can be made in the process parameters in unit operation to eliminate or reduce the risk. Real time monitoring of the process provides early signs of risk and can be avoided by appropriate measures.

Risk Priority Number (RPN)

The probability or occurrence, severity and detectability of each risk has to be assessed, hence, a value is assigned to each factor on a scale of 1 to 10. The definition for each number has to be made so that the assignment of a value is constant. When low, medium and high are used to assign value they are translated into 1, 3 and 5 on a 1-5 scale. This exercise is required so that all risks can be compared numerically to prioritize the risks.

Probability: Estimate how frequently the failure mode is likely to occur. Scores are typically from 1 (rare) to 10 (frequent).

Severity: Assign a score (1 to 10) indicating the potential impact on product quality or patient safety.

Detectability: Rate the ease with which the failure mode can be detected before it affects the product. Scores range from 1 (easily detected) to 10 (difficult to detect).

Risk Priority Number (RPN) is the product of all three values of probability, severity and detectability. For example, Probability is 5, severity is 7 and detectability is 3 then the RPN is equal to 5x7x3=105.

Risk Acceptance

It is not possible always to eliminate the risk even after implementing best possible mitigation actions and the risk still exists but at a lower level. Risk acceptance is a decision to accept at certain level. For example, an impurity level is high (1.0%) but it has been reduced to low level (0.1%) by mitigation actions and regulatory acceptance is 0.2%. Then risk acceptance level of not more than 0.15% may be considered. The risk acceptance level is decided on case-by-case basis. The risk acceptance level is considered only after making best efforts to eliminate the risk.

3.3 Risk Communication

Risk communication is the process of sharing information about risks related to pharmaceutical product development and manufacturing with relevant parties. The stake holders are internal departments of industry, regulators, patients and health professionals. The communication about the nature, probability, severity, detectability, treatment, and any other aspect of quality of risk to other relevant party is important. It is not necessary to communicate each risk to all the stake holders but communication to only relevant party is essential. The dotted lines in Figure 3.1 indicates communication process between parties while the solid lines indicate the communication and documentation of QRM.

The very purpose of risk communication to relevant parties is to get their insights and expert opinion on the risk. The recommendations of a party have to be considered in reducing the risk further by implementing appropriate changes. It should also be noted that the resources required to eliminate or further reduce the risk may be huge and the outcome may not be practically useful. Hence, the risk review is made critically to take appropriate decisions whether to implement changes or to accept the risk at that level.

3.4 Risk Reviews

Risk review is a crucial process that involves systematically identifying, evaluating, and managing potential risks associated with product development and manufacturing. Risk review is an ongoing process and the frequency of review depends on the level of the risk. The mitigation plans for risk elimination or reduction are implemented and the outcome of actions taken is reviewed to assess the reduction in the risk. The risk acceptance level is revised based on the results for continuous improvement in the process.

The risk review also should consider the possibility of new risks due to implementation of change in process parameters, material attributes and analytical methodology. It means while addressing an identified risk with some changes in the process parameters may create new risk(s) that is not considered earlier. Hence, the review process should be holistic and consider afresh to identify, evaluate and control risks after implementation of changes to the existing process.

Risk review is a continuous process throughout the life cycle of drug product. The data review, audit reports, inspection reports etc., are used to gain more knowledge about the product and process to reduce the risks.

3.5 Risk Management Methodology

Risk is assessed by assigning a value to the probability, severity and detectability of risk with prior knowledge, expertise and scientific tools. Informal procedures such as standard operating procedures (SOPs) were used earlier wherein the trend data, charts, and the results were used to identify and mitigate risks.

For example, water content of finished product more than 3.0% found to increase the hydrolytic impurity of drug. The possible causes and mitigation plans are prepared by the cross functional team based on SOP.

Possible Cause	**Mitigation Plan**
Water content of input material	Select excipients with low water content
Fluid uptake during RMG granulation	Optimize the fluid uptake
Drying conditions	Optimize the drying process to control water content below 3.0%
Relative humidity (RH) of Manufacturing area	Maintain low RH in the production area

The above empirical or knowledge-based approach depends on the prior knowledge and expertise of the people involved.

Quality Risk Management is a scientific and practical approach that utilizes well documented, transparent and reliable methods for risk management and informed decision. Various QRM tools are available that provide a step-by-step process to identify, assess and mitigate the risk. The following tools are regularly used but several other tools are also available and equally useful.

- Ishikawa or fish bone diagram
- Failure Mode Effects Analysis (FMEA) and Failure Mode, Effects Criticality Analysis (FMECA)
- Fault Tree Analysis (FTA)
- Preliminary Hazard Analysis (PHA)
- Hazard Operability Analysis (HAZOP)
- Hazard Analysis and Critical Control Points (HACCP)
- Probabilistic Risk Assessment (PRA)
- Risk Ranking and Filtering (RRF)
- Supporting Statistical Tools

Ishikawa or Fish Bone Diagram

Kaoru Ishikawa has developed the process of identifying the cause for the effect observed and is called cause-effect diagram and also Ishikawa diagram or fish bone diagram since the diagram looks like a fish bone **Figure 3.2**. This tool can be used prospectively to identify the risk or retrospectively for root cause analysis. The structure of the diagram is essentially built on question "why" a particular effect and this process is continued till there is no further assignable cause.

The effect or risk is represented at the end of an arrow. The possible causes are first divided into Materials, Machines, Manpower, Method, Measurement and Mother nature and in short, they are called 6M.

1. *Materials:* All the raw materials used as input in the process have to be investigated for their procurement, storage, quality standard, dispensing, intermediate storage and their appropriate use in the process.
2. *Machines:* The use of right machine, its preventive maintenance, calibration, and operation conditions.
3. *Manpower:* The people skill set, training, understanding of critical steps, attitude and working habits.
4. *Method:* Method here refers to the processes followed. Review of each unit operation, documentation, and quality of output of each unit operation.
5. *Measurement:* Means the analytical methods used to determine certain quality parameter, selectivity, precision, and robustness. Standards used in the measurement and sample preparation.
6. *Mother nature:* Refers to the environment in which the activities are conducted. The temperature, relative humidity, cleanliness, and control of material and men movement.

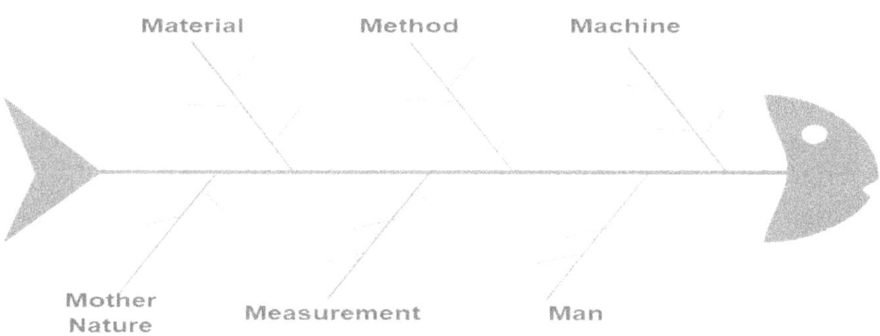

Figure 3.2 Ishikawa or Fish Bone diagram of 6Ms.

Each 'M' has been drawn as a main branch and now each 'M' is further evaluated to find out possible cause and is presented on main branch as a sub-branch. The sub-branch can be further divided into fine bones to represent the elements that contribute to the cause. An example of Ishikawa diagram for the risk of high-water content in finished product is presented in **Figure 3.3**.

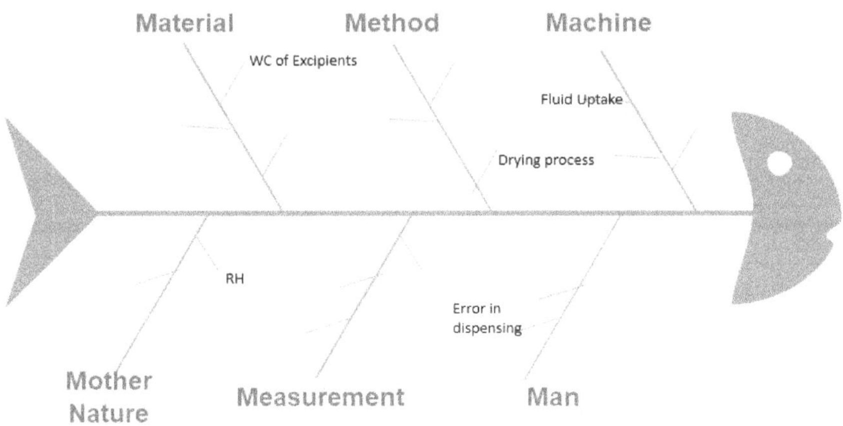

Figure 3.3 Probable causes of high-water content in the finished product.

The identified causes for the presence of high-water content in the product are now subjected for analysis and evaluation to come up with mitigation plans.

Failure Mode Effects Analysis (FMEA) and Failure Mode, Effects Criticality Analysis (FMECA)

This is a proactive process before conducting any experiment and collecting data. The proposed composition and/or process is subjected for FMEA. The possible failure modes are identified by questioning 'what can go wrong?' and what are the effects of the failure? Hence, FMEA is a risk assessment tool used within the Quality by Design (QbD) framework to proactively identify potential failure modes in a process, assess their potential impact, and prioritize them for mitigation.

FMEA is based on brain storming by cross functional team members in identifying, analysing and evaluating the risks. This a step-by-step process involving documentation, transparency, and communication between the members. The following steps are followed in conducting FMEA and FMECA process. The key difference between FMEA and FMECA is that FMECA includes the criticality of the failure mode by assessing the severity, occurrence and detectability quantitatively. Hence, the steps 7 to 10 are related to FMECA and all other steps are common to both FMEA and FMECA.

1. ***Selection of product or process or system for FMEA***

   The process owner of the FMEA should define the scope clearly to make the process very effective. This includes defining boundaries, objectives, and justification for the analysis. For example, understanding the failure mode that affects water content in the tablet based on the proposed composition and process, and finalizing the specification.

2. ***Creation of cross functional team members***

   The purpose of building a cross functional team is to ensure that all risk areas are considered by each relevant department experts. For example, members from formulation, analytical, process, technology transfer, developmental quality assurance, and finance departments are relevant in drug product development.

3. ***Review of the issue***

   In order to analyse the issue, it is necessary to present the composition of the product, process flow diagram, details of equipment used, and current controls available. This information helps the members to think critically about the potential failure modes.

4. ***Identification of potential failure modes***

   The team members should express the failure mode without any justification so that a list of failure modes is identified. There is no discussion on the failure mode identified at this stage so that members are free to propose any hypothetical failure mode. Use brainstorming, technical expertise, and historical data to generate a thorough list.

5. ***Assessment of effect of each failure mode***

   Consider the effect on product performance, user safety, regulatory compliance, and business operations. This is the stage where each failure mode is reviewed critically by cross functional team to finalize the list of failure modes.

6. ***Identification of potential causes for failure modes***

   The possible cause or causes for each failure mode have to be identified. Analysing each cause to deeper level is important to find out the root cause. Identifying causes accurately is key to selecting effective mitigation strategies.

7. ***Assigning the rating to probability, severity and detectability of failure mode***

   At this step, ratings have to be given to each failure mode for probability, severity and detectability. Prior knowledge, expertise, and available data are used to assign rating to these three factors of a risk.

8. ***Determination of RPN for each failure mode and ranking the RPN***

   The values of probability, severity, and detectability assigned to each failure mode are documented in tabular form. RPN value of each failure mode is calculated and entered into the table. The RPN values are now arranged from highest value to lowest value.

9. ***Prioritization of actions based on the ranking of RPN***

   The ranking of RPN values are used to prioritize the failure modes for whom mitigation plans are required. High RPN values demand for mitigation plans to avoid failure mode and risk.

10. ***Implementation of mitigation actions***

    The cause or causes of failure mode are used to decide actions for eliminating or reducing the failure mode. The efforts are made to reduce probability and severity and/or to improve detectability.

11. ***Re-assessment of RPN after implementation of mitigation actions***

    The cross functional team should meet and assign new values to probability, severity and detectability based on the current status after implementation of mitigation actions. The RPN is recalculated with new assigned values and documented. If the revised RPN is still a concern, further mitigation actions may be implemented till the failure mode RPN is acceptable.

12. ***Identification of new failure modes if any due to implementation of mitigation plans***

    In certain cases, implementation of mitigation actions may reduce a particular failure mode but the implemented actions may lead to new failure mode(s). Hence, a thorough FMEA is required post implementation of mitigation plans.

13. ***Documentation and continuous assessment periodically***

    FMEA document is not static but dynamic throughout the life cycle of the product. Hence, a periodic review of FMEA is practiced and revised with proper documentation.

Fault Tree Analysis (FTA)

FTA is a top down process where a problem or failure mode or unwanted outcome is placed on the top and the causes are drilled down. Each cause is further analysed to sub-causes and sub-causes are further broken into basic causes. The diagram looks like an inverted tree. The causes, sub-causes and basic causes are analysed qualitatively and quantitatively and are the basis for the mitigation plans. The diagram is prepared by using symbols that carry meaning to that event and AND or OR are used to represent the reason for the event. The AND operator indicates occurrence of event due to more than one event while OR represent alternative possibilities for same event **Figure 3.4**.

The symbols and meaning of each symbol are explained below.

 Circle represents the basic event

 Diamond represents undeveloped event

 Rectangular represents intermediate event

 House represents normal event

 Ellipse represents conditioning event

 OR symbol

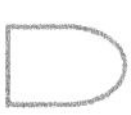 AND symbol

Basic events: The fault tree analysis ends with basic events that are like leaves of a tree. They are represented by circle and the combination of basic events lead to intermediate event (Fault). The basic events are considered for quantitative assessment by assigning a failure rate or value.

Undeveloped event: It is graphically represented by diamond. An undeveloped event is an event that is not considered in the fault tree analysis either because it is unimportant or sufficient evidence is not available to consider.

Intermediate event: An intermediate event is always a fault that is a result of logical combination of other events occurring down the tree. Since intermediate events are caused by other events, they are almost always a type of logical gate. It is represented by rectangle.

Normal events: Normal events are part of nominal behaviour of the system and do not represent any fault. These events are represented by a house symbol in the flow diagram.

Conditioning event: This event serves as a special condition or constraint for certain types of gates and does not represent any fault. A conditioning event is represented by an ellipse.

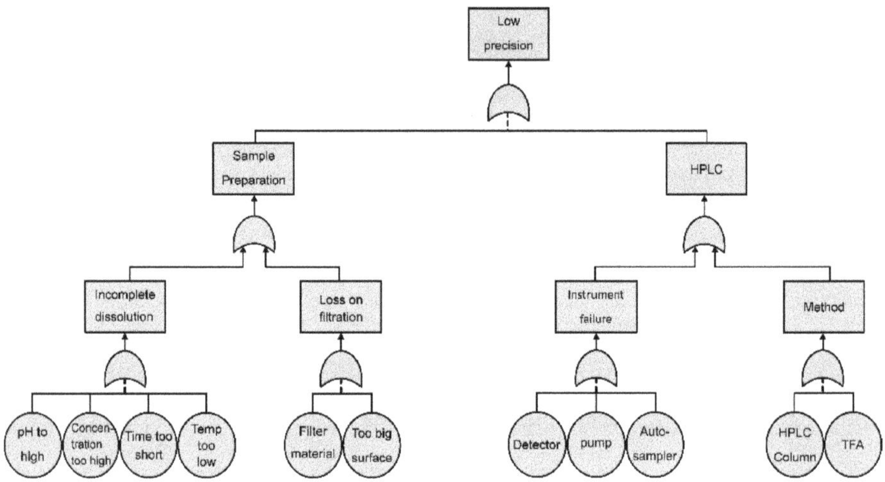

Figure 3.4 Fault Tree Analysis.

Preliminary Hazard Analysis (PHA)

PHA is a proactive initial analysis of possible hazards or failure modes in the process or system based on prior experience or knowledge of hazard or failure. It involves identification of future hazard and qualitative assessment of extent of damage or harm that would result. Relative ranking of hazards based on probability and severity is carried out and also possible mitigation plans are proposed. PHA is carried out before the initiation of the process or system where little information is available about process or system and the identified hazards are further analysed by other QRM tools.

Hazard Operability Analysis (HAZOP)

HAZOP based on a theory that assumes that risk events are caused by deviations from the design or operating intentions. It is highly useful in manufacturing process whether internal or out sourced. The primary objective of HAZOP is to identify critical process parameters that would lead to occurrence of hazard. The expert in the field are assembled and brain storm on the identification of critical points that would result in hazard or quality failure if deviate from operational ranges. It has also been used primarily in the pharmaceutical industry for evaluating process safety hazards. The output of a HAZOP analysis is a list of critical operations for risk management. This facilitates regular monitoring of critical points in the manufacturing process.

Hazard Analysis and Critical Control Points (HACCP)

HACCP is most useful when product and process understanding is sufficiently comprehensive to support identification of critical control points. It is a systematic, proactive and preventive tool used to ensure product quality, safety and reliability. Technical tools and scientific principles are applied step-by-step to identify, analyse, evaluate, prevent, and control the hazard or adverse consequences of hazard that arise due to design, development, production, and use of products. The steps involved in HACCP are:

1. Hazard analysis of each step of process to identify probable hazard, analyse and identify preventive measure(s).
2. Identify critical control points that have to be monitored to avoid occurrence of hazard.
3. Establish critical limits for controls within which the operation should happen.
4. Create a system to monitor the critical control points within the limits.
5. Establish the corrective action when critical control points are out of the limits.
6. The HACCP system has to be thoroughly verified to estimate it's working efficiency.
7. Good documentation and record keeping is required for healthy implementation of HACCP.

Probabilistic Risk Assessment (PRA)

PRA is a group of techniques that incorporate variability and uncertainty into the risk assessment process. It provides estimates of the range and likelihood of a hazard, exposure or risk, rather than a single point estimate. QbD emphasizes building quality into the product from the initial design stages rather than relying solely on end-product testing. PRA aligns with this by providing a framework to quantify and understand the variability and uncertainty associated with potential risks throughout the product lifecycle. PRA uses mathematical and statistical methods to assign numerical probabilities to potential risks and their consequences. This enables a more precise evaluation of risk and helps prioritize mitigation efforts.

Variability in critical process parameters (CPPs) influence the CQAs of the drug product and hence, PRA quantifies the variability and proposes range of CPPs within which the quality is maintained. The data is analysed by Monte Carlo simulations to assess uncertainty of the event or hazard.

Risk Ranking and Filtering (RRF)

RRF involves breaking down complex risks into smaller, more manageable components and evaluating them based on predefined criteria to determine their impact and likelihood. Both qualitative and quantitative risks are analysed using common risk ranking procedure so that all type of risks are ranked form high risk to low risk to enable decision makers to allocate appropriate resources to maintain safety, efficacy and quality of product. Risk ranking methods are particularly helpful in situations in which the portfolio of risks and the underlying consequences to be managed are diverse and difficult to compare using a single tool.

Filtering is a process of removing some risks based on the weighting factors or cut-off value of RPN number or risk score. The purpose of this activity is to avoid unimportant risks from the list and keep high risks for management attention so that effective measures can be taken to manage the risks.

Supporting Statistical Tools

QRM is supported by several statistical tools to make scientific and informed decisions. Several statistical tools are available for this purpose but most routinely used tools are discussed here.

1. Control Charts
2. Histograms
3. Pareto analysis
4. Design of Experiments (DoE)
5. Process Capability Analysis

Control Charts: Control charts are maintained by measuring a CQA for each batch when batch to batch variation is considered. The CQA is plotted per each batch and the trend is analysed. They help visualize process behaviour over time, identify deviations from expected performance, and trigger corrective actions when necessary. In addition, the possible root cause for observed deviation of the CQA value in a particular batch can be assessed and preventive measures can be implemented. The process understanding improves and process stability is assessed **Figure 3.5**.

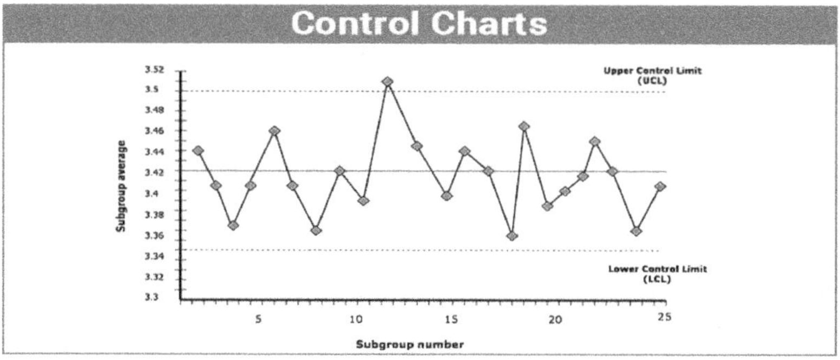

Figure 3.5 Control chart of CQA for the batches manufactured over time.

Histograms: Histograms are constructed by plotting the group or class versus the frequency of occurrence of that group or class. For example, disintegration time (DT) or weight of tablet is measured for 100 tablets and the data obtained is divided into a group. Let us consider the DT values for creating a histogram **Table 3.1 & Figure 3.6**.

Table 3.1 DT of tablets and frequency.

Group	DT in min	Frequency%
1	<3	1
2	3.1-4.0	8
3	4.1-5.0	35
4	5.1-6.0	40
5	6.1-7.0	10
6	7.1-8.0	5
7	>8	1

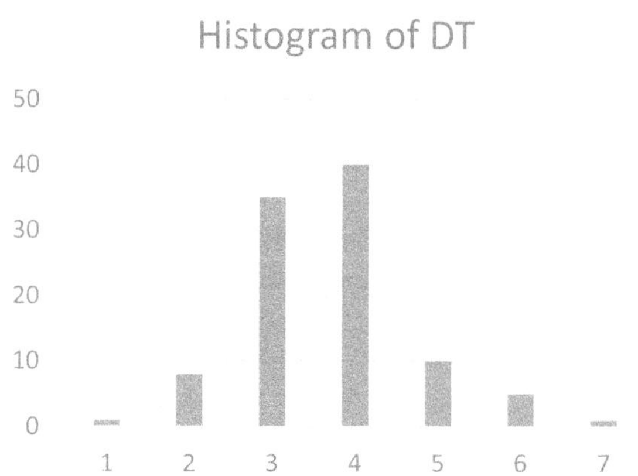

Figure 3.6 Histogram of disintegration time of tablets.

Histograms provide a visual representation of the frequency distribution of data, making it easy to understand the shape of the distribution (e.g., normal, skewed, bimodal). Histograms can highlight data points that fall outside the expected range, indicating potential outliers or unusual occurrences. Histograms can be used to compare the output of different processes or the same process under different conditions, allowing for the identification of differences in their performance.

Pareto Analysis: It is based on the idea that 80 percent of problems may be caused by as few as 20 percent of causes and also called 80/20 rule. Therefore, by addressing the 20% causes of failure 80% of problems are resolved. Pareto analysis can be applied to manufacturing defects or failure to meet specifications of a drug product. For example, analysis of the data identified that 80% of defects are due to weight variation of tablets while 20% defects are from other factors. In this case, the tablet weight variation would be considered a "vital few" factor, and the company would focus its quality improvement efforts on addressing the causes of this specific defect, such as optimizing the tablet press settings or improving raw material consistency.

Design of Experiments (DoE): DOE is a statistical method used to plan and conduct experiments to determine the relationships between input variables (material attributes, process parameters) and output responses (quality attributes). The data analysis by statistical tools enables the scientist to identify critical material attributes (CMAs) and critical process parameters (CPPs) that impact critical quality attributes (CQAs) of the product. Optimisation of CPPs would help to create design space within which the CQAs are always maintained within the specified limits. A detailed discussion on DoE is presented in another chapter of this book.

Process Capability Analysis: It quantifies how well a process meets predefined specifications, identifying potential issues and guiding process improvements. When a design space is established for a process, the process parameters are fixed at its centre so that the product quality is at its best. Process Capability (cp) is the measure of quality of product meeting its specifications when the process is carried out with the process parameters at the centre of design space. Process Capability Index (cpk) measures the effect of spread of process parameters within the design space. It means, the process parameters are intentionally varied from the centre of design space to the periphery of design space and the quality of the product should meet its specifications. Taguchi Capability Index (cpm) is a measure of ability of design space in producing the product with target quality. This index assesses the predictability of design space in achieving desired quality of product.

CHAPTER 4

Factors Affecting Generic Product Design

Generic product design depends on several factors unlike product design of new chemical entity. The generic product design should consider innovator design, API selection, excipients selection, dosage form, patent landscape, cost of product, product stability, bioequivalence, regulatory requirements and company capabilities. This chapter presents in detail discussion of each factor in finalising the generic product design by the formulation department in consultation with cross functional teams.

4.1 Innovator Product Design

Generic product is always evaluated in comparison with the innovator product and it should exhibit similar safety, efficacy and quality compared to innovator product also called reference listed drug (RLD). The new chemical entity or existing drug substance is formulated by innovator company into a suitable dosage form to achieve QTPP.

The first step in designing generic product is to understand RLD design and performance by studying literature and evaluating the RLD by various techniques. Reverse engineering of RLD is carried out thoroughly to get answers to the following questions.

1. **What type of dosage form is RLD?**

   The type of dosage form influences the generic product design since some dosage forms may demand similar product design. For example, drug leaded pellets are filled into a capsule by the innovator. Deviation from pellet formulation is difficult since multi-particulate system exhibits different drug release and bioavailability compared with single unit formulation. Therefore, the generic product design should consider this point and if patent on dosage form exists, then mini tablets in place of pellets with appropriate drug release control may be considered.

2. **What strengths are marketed? What is the size of highest strength?**

   Number of strengths marketed by innovator are considered to develop generic product with similar strengths. The size of the highest strength has to be reviewed. If any linear dimension of dosage form is equal to or greater than 17mm, then size and shape guidance of FDA indicates that generic product dimensions should not exceed the RLD dosage form dimensions. Shape should be convenient to swallow.

In addition, bioequivalence study is conducted with one strength and other strengths are eligible for biowaiver if they meet the regulatory requirements. Therefore, the generic product should either have dose proportional composition or look-a-like composition to avail biowaiver for other strengths. This imposes a serious constraint in designing generic drug product.

3. **What is the polymorphic form of API used in the formulation?**

   A drug substance may exist in more than one polymorphic form and each polymorphic form may have different physicochemical properties. Hence, the generic development should consider appropriate polymorphic form for stability and bioavailability. Deviation from polymorphic form used by innovator poses challenges and appropriate composition and process should be used to address the challenges.

4. **What is the Particle size distribution (PSD) and crystal habit of API in dosage form**?

   BCS class II and IV APIs are highly sensitive to PSD and crystal habit with respect to processibility, stability and dissolution from dosage form. If due to patent constraint the PSD of API used in generic product is higher then use of surfactants may support dissolution.

5. **What is the BCS class of API?**

   Biopharmaceutics Classification System (BCS) is highly useful in understanding the in-vivo behaviour of drug. BCS class I and III drugs are highly soluble and do not pose much problem in dissolution while BCS II and IV drugs are poorly soluble and the bioavailability of these drug is limited by dissolution. If permeability of drug is considered, then BCS class I and II are highly permeable while BCS III & IV drugs have low permeability. Hence, BCS class I drugs pose less problem in bioequivalence and BCS class II drugs bioavailability can be achieved by mapping dissolution of generic product in biorelevant media. BCS III drugs dissolution is not an issue but permeability is low and hence, generic formulator has to just map the dissolution and pay attention to permeability enhancers to achieve bioequivalence with RLD. BCS class IV drugs have low solubility and permeability leading to high variability in bioavailability and hence, establishing bioequivalence for this class is challenging.

6. **What are the excipients used in the formulation? And in what quantities?**

   Qualitative (Q1) and quantitative (Q2) composition of innovator product is useful in understanding the compatibility of excipients with drug and the functionality of each excipients and its significance in the formulation. Generic product should contain as par as possible similar excipients and in same quantity. However, if a change in either qualitative or quantitative composition of one or more excipients is inevitable due to patents, cost, non-availability of reliable supplier then selection of alternative excipient is critical.

7. **What is the design of RLD? What is the three-dimensional arrangement of drug and excipients in dosage form?**

   The three-dimensional arrangement (Q3) of drug and excipients control the stability and drug release kinetics both in-vitro and in-vivo. Let consider an example of drug pellets designed for controlled release. **Figure 4.1** provides the details of the innovator product design. Sugar spheres are used and drug is layered on it using HPMC 3cps followed by citric acid layer in HPMC. The rate controlling layer consist of ethylcellulose, dibutyl phthalate and organic solvent. The thickness of each layer can be measured using scanning electron microscope (SEM) of cut pellet.

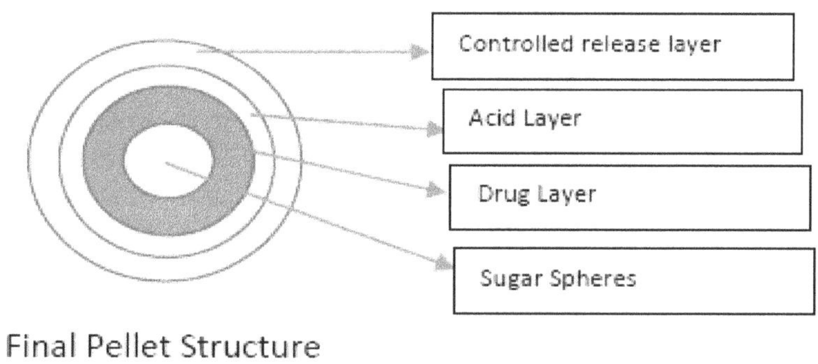

Figure 4.1 Three-dimensional arrangement of drug and excipients.

The generic product design should try to mimic the innovator design with required modification due to patents.

8. **What process steps are involved in the manufacture of RLD?**

   It is difficult but necessary to understand the process steps involved in the manufacture of innovator product so that generic product process is close to that of innovator. In the above example, it can be understood that the pellet is manufactured using Fluid Bed Coater (FBC) by Wurster process.

9. **What packing configuration is used?**

   In case of blisters, the packing material of construction, thickness, and pouch size of innovator product is a guiding principle for selection of blister packing for generic product. Similarly, innovator bottle pack evaluation has to be carried out with respect to material of construction (MOC), thickness of wall, total volume, type of cap and vapour permeation of bottle. The data generated would help in selecting suitable packing material for generic product.

10. **What is the cost of RLD?**

    Cost plays a significant role in generic product portfolio. The selection of a product for generic development depends on the breadth of markets, cost of product, profit margin and volume of sales. However, the generic drug product target cost is expected to be between 1-5% of innovator cost for viability. The lower the cost of generic drug product, the more successful in market and also benefits patients financially. In addition, the product can combat with other generic companies.

4.2 Patents on Active Pharmaceutical Ingredient (API)

Intellectual property rights are very important in current business environment. Companies invest huge amount of money and resources for inventing new drugs for a specific disease or improving manufacturing process for better yields or quality or to create new polymorphs of existing drugs. Based on the invention different types of patents are granted to the inventors and this blocks the generic companies using such patented drug substances. The important types of patents related to API are discussed.

Compound Patents: In general, new chemical entities (NCEs) are patented for the molecule structure and this is the strongest form of protection for the invention. The patent term is 20 years during which no other person or company is allowed to use the invention. This type of patent provides exclusive rights to manufacture, sell, use, and import the chemical for any use. Designing around the patent is not possible and hence, generic company has to wait till the expiry of the patent. The only legal path available is to invalidate the patent based on prior art.

Isomer patents: Drug substance may exist as different stereoisomers and one of them may have better therapeutic activity than other isomers. The isomer having highest therapeutic benefit is patented though the original patent related to drug substance is expired. For example, Omeprazole is a racemic mixture of (S)-omeprazole and (R)-omeprazole which are enantiomers. (S)-omeprazole is also called as Esomperazole provides best therapeutic benefit compared with (R)-omeprazole due to its slow metabolism and reliable bioavailability. Therefore, Esomeprazole is patented by the innovator and blocked the entry of generics for several years.

Process Patents: The manufacturing process for the production of API is patented in which the key starting material (KSM) and subsequent steps are patented. In general, the most cost effective manufacturing is patented to have cost advantage. These patents can be circumvented by inventing alternate routes of synthesis other than the patented process. Though this type of patents is not blocking the generic companies but puts lot of stress by blocking easy and cost-effective manufacturing process.

Method of Use Patents: The use of NCE in treating a specific disease(s) is patented including the dose and dosing regimen. This type of patent can also be obtained for old drugs by identifying new use of drugs called repurposing. For example, use of Aspirin as an anti-coagulant is a new indication while the old indication is for pain and fever. This type of patents is difficult to invalidate unless substantial prior art is available in the public domain.

Solid state and PSD patents: Some drug substances exist in different polymorphic form that exhibit different physicochemical properties especially stability and dissolution. Hence, generic companies have to use different polymorphic form that is not covered in the patent. This requires development of new polymorphic form by generic companies or use of polymorphic form not patented by innovator or any other company. For example, esomeprazole magnesium trihydrate form is patented that has better stability. Generic companies have used unstable amorphous form by stabilizing it using appropriate stabilizer in the composition.

Particle size distribution of drug is very critical for inhalation product and the ideal PSD is having D50 value of 1 to 5 um. If this range is patented by the innovator, then the only way left to generic company is to invalidate the patent.

Product-by-Process Patents: These patents cover a product specifically when it can be distinguished from its competitors only by the method used to manufacture it. In this case, the patented method of manufacture should be avoided and an alternative method has to be used.

Miscellaneous Patents: Solid dispersion and spray drying techniques are used to convert crystalline API into stable amorphous form and the inventions are patented. Co-crystals of drugs are also patented since co-crystals are considered as API as per FDA guidance.

It can be concluded that API manufacturer should consider all the types of patents for a particular drug and come up with non-infringing strategy to synthesize, crystallize, and mill to provide desired PSD.

4.3 Patents on Formulation, Process and others

The drug product is a result of composition and process used to manufacture it. The composition refers to qualitative (Q1) and Quantitative (Q2) and most importantly three dimensional arrangements of drug and various excipients with the help of a suitable process. Modern pharmaceutics has invented several drug delivery systems and dosage forms for achieving best therapeutic benefit to the patients. Hence, not only the therapeutic moiety is important but also the design of drug delivery system for best therapeutic outcome. In solid oral tablets, the innovation spans from a simple immediate release tablets to site specific controlled release drug delivery system. Similarly, many novel drug delivery systems are developed for different routes of administration. Many patents are granted for composition, process and combination thereof. Generic product development considers the patents on these domains and comes up with design around strategies. It should be noted that development of non-infringing strategy is applicable only when a generic company likes to market the product well before the expiry of the existing patents (innovator or third party).

Formulation Patents: This type of patents protects the unique combination of active ingredients and excipients, carriers or delivery mechanisms in a drug product. The inventions limit the use of certain functional excipients, and the quantities of excipients by generic companies. Generic product development has to come up alternative formulation designs that would still perform similar to that of RLD. These patents allow innovators to differentiate their products and maintain a competitive edge, even after the initial patent on the active ingredient has expired. For example, diffCORE technology utilizes enteric coating and part of the enteric coating is removed during the manufacturing **Figure 4.2**. Now the drug release happens in stomach through the surface of core tablet where enteric coating is removed. The generic company has to come up with a strategy that mimics the drug release pattern similar to diffCORE technology based tablet. The possible design is to use highly water soluble plasticizer in the coating that will get dissolved quickly creating small pores throughout the coating membrane. Optimization of coating material to plasticizer ratio would provide the composition having similar dissolution profiles to that of RLD.

Other examples are Extended-release versions of drugs for improved patient compliance, specialized coatings for better stability, or novel drug delivery systems like transdermal patches or nanoparticle formulations.

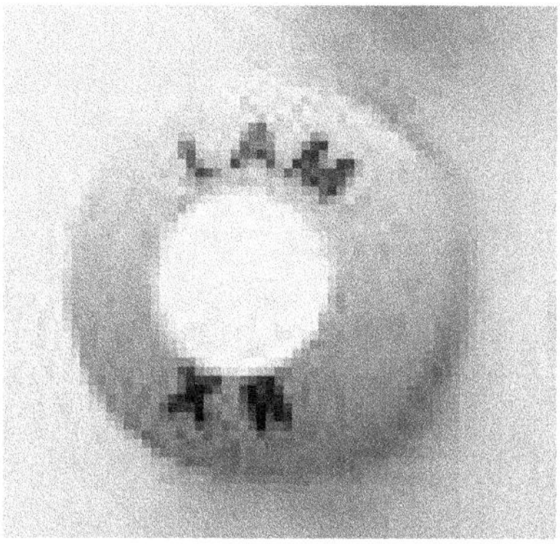

Figure 4.2 DiffCORE technology for controlled delivery.

Process Patents: Drug product manufacturing patents provide pharmaceutical companies with exclusive rights to their inventions, incentivizing innovation and allowing them to recoup research and development costs. The process for the manufacture of a drug product is patented by the innovator so that generic companies have to find another process to manufacture the product. These type of patents are relatively weak and alternate process can be developed. However, the process selected should be capable of producing product that exhibit similar stability, dissolution and bioavailability.

Method of Use Patents: These patents are a key tool for drug repurposing and lifecycle management, allowing companies to extend market exclusivity for new indications of existing drugs. The dose and dosage regimen of drug product is claimed in the patents. It is difficult to design non-infringing strategy since dose and dosage regimen can't be different for a generic drug product. The only way is to challenge the patents based on prior art and invalidating the patent.

Product-by-Process Patents: The product by process patents are those patents where a product is claimed from a specific process to manufacture. DiffCORE technology based product comes in this category where a special tablet design is claimed using diffCORE technology process.

Miscellaneous: Solid dispersion technology is used to prepare amorphous form of drug in which a carrier is used to stabilize the amorphous form of drug. Various carriers and their ratio with drug are claimed along with process conditions. Similarly, spry drying technology and hot melt extrusion are also used to produce amorphous form of drug. Generic companies have to come up with different methodology to prepare and stabilize amorphous form of drug. Use of amorphous form of drug directly and stabilizing it in the formulation is one of the non-infringing strategy. The challenge is to stabilize the amorphous form in the dosage form on stability and achieving dissolution and bioequivalence.

4.4 Regulatory Requirements

Regulatory agencies have issued several guidance for the quality control of drug products. The drug product development should keep regulatory requirements in consideration in the development and manufacturing of drug products. The list of requirements starts with drug substance and continuous after commercialization of the product.

1. Drug substance
2. Excipients
3. Residual Solvents
4. Development
5. Container and closure system
6. Stability
7. Manufacturing
8. Quality Control (QC) and Quality Assurance (QA)
9. Good Documentation Practices (GDP)

Drug Substance: The drug substance selected should be supplied by FDA approved manufacturing company having drug master file (DMF) filed with US FDA or active substance master file (ASMF) in Europe or appropriate filing in target country. The API should meet monograph of pharmacopoeia of the geography and if no monograph exists for the drug substance, then it should meet general requirements for drug substance in that geography.

Excipients: For excipients, an equivalent to the standard pharmaceutical Drug Master File (DMF) is typically a Type IV DMF in the US, or a national Excipient Master File (EMF) or customized approach in other countries like China, Canada, Japan, Australia, and India. Type IV DMF is the specific DMF type designated for excipients, colorants, flavours, and essences, allowing manufacturers to submit proprietary manufacturing details to the FDA without revealing them to the drug product manufacturer. Other relevant documents include a Certificate of Suitability (CEP) for excipients with

European Pharmacopoeia (Ph. Eur.) monographs, or a Plasma Master File (PMF) for human-derived materials like albumin.

Transmissible spongiform encephalopathies (TSEs), a group of diseases affecting the brain and nervous system in animals and humans. TSEs are characterized by the degeneration of brain tissue, leading to a spongy appearance, and are caused by abnormal proteins called prions. Prions are proteins that can fold into abnormal shapes, and these misfolded proteins can induce other proteins to misfold as well, leading to a cascade of misfolding and ultimately causing the disease. Bovine spongiform encephalopathy (BSE), is specific TSE that affects cattle and is commonly known as "mad cow disease". Hence, API and excipient manufacturer issues TSE and BSE certificates that confirms the product or its components do not contain any materials derived from animals that could potentially transmit transmissible spongiform encephalopathies (TSEs), including bovine spongiform encephalopathy (BSE).

Elemental impurities in drug products may arise from several sources; they may be residual catalysts that were added intentionally in synthesis or may be present as impurities (e.g., through interactions with processing equipment or container/closure systems or by being present in components of the drug product). Because elemental impurities do not provide any therapeutic benefit to the patient, their levels in the drug product should be controlled within acceptable limits. An Elemental Impurities Certificate from an excipient manufacturing company is a document that confirms the absence or controlled levels of specific elemental impurities in an excipient, as per regulatory guidelines.

The FDA restricts the amount of synthetic iron oxides in ingested drugs to 5 milligrams per day, calculated as elemental iron. This limit is found in regulations for colour additives.

Packing components should be procured from supplier who has filed Type III DMF with FDA which focuses on packaging components that come into direct contact with the drug product such as bottles, vials, blister packs and closures.

Inactive Ingredient Guide (IIG) is an official document that provides the maximum daily dose permitted for an excipient for a specific route of administration. Hence, the quantity of the excipients selected for drug product development should be within the permitted limits. Generally Regarded as Safe (GRAS) materials are those whose intake is considered safe for a particular route of administration and generally these materials are used in food. Special attention has to be paid to the grades of an excipient since the IIG limits differ for each grade of excipients.

Residual Solvents: Solvents are chemicals in liquid state that are used in the manufacture of API and Excipients and removed from the product finally. However, there may be solvents still present in the drug or excipient called residual solvents. Sometimes, solvents are also used in drug manufacturing process which are also removed but traces of solvents may present in the drug product. These solvents are hazardous to the animal or human health and hence, regulatory guidance provides permitted daily exposure (PDE) based on the harm the solvent causes and its concentration. The residual solvents are classified based on their impact on the health of animal, human, and environment.

Class 1: Solvents with unacceptable toxicity or environmental hazards belongs to Class 1 and they have to removed completely from the drug product. Examples, carbon tetrachloride and benzene.

Class 2: These solvents have inherent toxicity but their amount has to be limited below threshold of their hazardous level. Examples, Acetonitrile and methanol.

Class 3: Solvents with low toxic potential comes under this category and the permitted limits are high. Examples, Ethanol and acetone.

Drug Product Development: Current development of drug products should include quality by design approach. The quality of product has to be built at every step of drug product development rather than testing finished product. All the guidance relevant to the dosage form such as size and shape, discriminatory dissolution test, IVIVC, design space and control strategy have to be considered during development. Scale independent process parameters can be optimized at lab scale but scale dependent process parameters have to be optimized at higher scale. Scale up of manufacturing process should consider engineering principles and operational range of critical process parameters have to be established.

Container and Closure System: Selection of container and closure system is a systematic, science-based approach to develop a suitable container and closure system that ensures product quality, safety, and efficacy throughout its lifecycle. In addition, inclusion of other materials such as desiccants and oxygen absorbing materials in bottles to protect drug product have to be considered. Child resistant closure systems are recommended to avoid accidental consumption of drug products by children. Device and product combinations should follow relevant guidance issued by regulatory authorities. Material of construction of packaging material may interact with the drug product leading stability and contamination by packaging materials. Leachables and extractables from packaging material into liquid preparations has be minimized.

Stability: Thorough review of physical and chemical properties of drug substance and drug product is carried out to identify the factors that influence the stability of drug product. The factors that influence the stability of drug product are controlled by selecting proper container and closure system and if required specific materials such as desiccant or oxygen scavenger are placed in the bottle. The drug product in proper container and closure system is placed in stability chambers maintained at specified temperature and humidity and analysed for CQAs at predetermined time points. The storage conditions for a drug product depends on the geography and dosage form.

Manufacturing: The manufacturing of drug products should follow current good manufacturing practices (cGMP). The facility, equipment, utilities, resources, documentation, testing, storage, and distribution activities should follow the current regulatory guidance. Identify factors that affect stability of drug product and select suitable container and closure system. The packing operation has to be optimized to ensure proper packing of drug product. The in-process quality control or process analytical technology should ensure smooth manufacturing of drug product. The process capability of the manufacturing process should be monitored regularly and continuous improvement of the process has to be made.

Quality Control (QC) and Quality Assurance (QA): Quality control in QbD shifts from traditional, end-product testing to a proactive, science-based approach that integrates quality into the entire product lifecycle. It involves identifying Critical Quality Attributes (CQAs) and Critical Process Parameters (CPPs), understanding their relationships through scientific experimentation, and establishing a dynamic Control Strategy to ensure product quality throughout manufacturing. This continuous quality assurance, often enabled by Process Analytical Technology (PAT), allows for in-process monitoring and real-time adjustments, leading to improved product consistency, reduced batch failures, and continuous improvement.

Quality Assurance (QA) plays a vital role within QbD framework by ensuring that the established quality principles and controls are rigorously followed throughout the product lifecycle, from development to manufacturing and beyond. QA facilitates continuous improvement by monitoring the manufacturing process, analysing performance data, and implementing necessary adjustments within the design space. This approach leads to more robust products, increased patient safety, streamlined regulatory processes, and improved operational efficiency.

Good Documentation Practices (GDP): Good Documentation Practices (GDP) involves a set of systematic procedures for preparing, reviewing, approving, issuing, recording, storing, and archiving documents, ensuring they are accurate, complete, legible, contemporaneous, traceable, original, and secure. Adherence to GDP in a QbD framework provides a reliable trail of data for regulatory compliance, demonstrates commitment to quality, minimizes errors, and enables informed decision-making for continuous improvement in the pharmaceutical and medical device industries.

4.5 Differentiated Products or 505B2 Products

Differentiated products or 505B2 products are neither new drug application (NDA) nor abbreviated new drug application (ANDA) but lie between these two applications. These products are submitted under "hybrid application" category in Europe. As per the FDA guidance, the following category of products are considered under 505B2 in US. 505(b)(2) drug products are approved by the FDA through a specific pathway that allows the applicant to rely on published data or data from previous studies on an already approved drug, in addition to their own studies of safety and effectiveness. Different types of differentiated products are listed below.

Active ingredient: An application for a change in an active ingredient such as a different salt, ester, complex, chelate, clathrate, racemate, or enantiomer of an active ingredient in a listed drug containing the same active moiety.

New molecular entity: In some cases, a new molecular entity may have been studied by parties other than the applicant and published information may be pertinent to the new application. This is particularly likely if the NME is the prodrug of an approved drug or the active metabolite of an approved drug. In some cases, data on a drug with similar pharmacologic effects could be considered critical to approval.

Naturally derived or recombinant active ingredient: An application for a drug product containing an active ingredient(s) derived from animal or botanical sources or recombinant technology where clinical investigations are necessary to show that the active ingredient is the same as an active ingredient in a listed drug.

Formulation: An application for a proposed drug product that contains a different quality or quantity of an excipient(s) than the listed drug where the studies required for approval are beyond those considered limited confirmatory studies appropriate to a 505(j) application. This approach is generally followed for injectable formulations.

Combination product: An application for a new combination product in which the active ingredients have been previously approved individually.

Dosing regimen: An application for a new dosing regimen, such as a change from twice daily to once daily.

New Indication: An application for a new indication not previously approved indication for a listed drug.

Rx/OTC switch: An application to change a prescription (Rx) indication to an over-the-counter (OTC) indication.

OTC monograph: An application for a drug product that differs from a product described in an OTC monograph (21 CFR 330.11), such as a non-monograph indication or a new dosage form.

Bioinequivalence: The proposed product has high rate and extent of absorption than the listed drug, and the applicant has conducted clinical trials to establish safety and efficacy of the product is eligible for marketing authorization under differentiated products.

The 505B2 products are also called as super generics since the requirements for these products is superior to ANDA but less compared with NDA of an NCE. Many companies around the World have been developing innovative products using existing drugs and they fall in any one of the types discussed above. 505B2 products pave a path for innovation in generic companies to bring drug products with benefit to patients that range from ease of administration to targeted drug delivery. Indian generic companies are not considering 505B2 products seriously and very few companies have brought innovative products into the market.

Ranbaxy: Bayer Pharma company is the innovator of Ciprofloxacin immediate release tablets and the dosage regimen is twice daily. Ranbaxy has developed extended release tablet of Ciprofloxacin and out licenced to Bayer Pharma. This is a great scientific success of an Indian company in 2001.

Lupin Ltd: Pitavastatin calcium (Brand: Livalo®) is developed by Kowa Company Limited, Japan for hydperlipidemia or mixed dyslipidemia as an adjunctive therapy to diet to reduce elevated total cholesterol, low-density lipoprotein cholesterol, apolipoprotein B, triglycerides and to increase high-density lipoprotein cholesterol. Lupin Limited, India has developed alternative salt Pitavastatin Sodium (Brand: Nikita®) and 1, 2, and 4mg tablets are marketed in USA.

Sun Pharma: Sun Pharma has developed few 505B2 products and got marketing authorization in US. Absorica™ is a lipid-based formulation in a hard gelatine capsule that offers better absorption in a fasted state compared to the original soft gel products (Roaccutane™/Accutane™).

Levetiracetam (Keppra®) developed by UCB pharma is used for anticonvulsant activity. Sun Pharma has developed extended release formulation using its patented wrap-matrix technology.

Abiraterone acetate (Zytiga®) is marketed by Johnson & Johnson for the treatment of of castrate resistant prostate cancer. A fixed dose combination of Abireterone acetate and methylprednisone is developed by Sun Pharma (YOSNA®).

Alembic Pharmaceuticals Ltd: Desvenlafaxine succinate (PRISTIQ®) extended release tablets were developed by Wyeth Laboratories for the treatment of depression. Alembic has developed extended release tablet using only base, Desvenlafaxine, that is bioequivalent to innovator product and got approval via 505B2 pathway. Later the product is licenced to Ranbaxy which was subsequently acquired by Sun Pharma.

Dr.Reddy;s Laboratories: A new injectable formulation of Palonosetron, an anti-emetic drug, with different buffer system and without EDTA has been developed for innovator injectable (ALOXI®).

A 505B2 application for Cyclophosphamide injection has been approved by USFDA wherein the composition is modified to give similar safety and efficacy compared to innovator product.

Bortezomib intravenous formulation is modified and filed under 505B2 route but discontinued later.

Promius Pharma: This is a subsidiary of Dr.Reddy's laboratories, focusing research on 505B2 products.

Betamethasone dipropionate (SERNIVO®) was developed as a spray (0.05%) for the treatment of mild to moderate plaque psoriasis. The product was launched in US in 2016.

Sumatriptan is used for the treatment of acute migraine attacks. Two different delivery systems were developed and out licensed to Upsher-Smith. Zembrace SynTouch® is 3mg strength injection while Tosymra® is a nasal spray 10mg.

Cipla: The FDA approval was based on a New Drug Application (NDA) submitted under the 505(b)(2) filing pathway. Lanreotide Injection is supplied in 60 mg/0.2 mL, 90 mg/0.3 mL, and 120 mg/0.5 mL single-dose pre-filled syringes. It is indicated for the treatment of patients with Acromegaly and Gastroenteropancreatic Neuroendocrine Tumors (GEP-NETs).

Cipla got approval for Leuprolide Acetate Injection Depot 22.5mg from USFDA based on an NDA submitted under 505b2 regulatory pathway.

4.6 Company Strategy and Facilities

Companies have specific strategies such as dosage form, therapeutic area, special population and geography. The generic product design depends on these strategies to support company growth. Some companies develop only one category of dosage forms such as solid orals, injectable, liposomes, extended release dosage forms, liquid orals, powder for oral solution/suspension, transdermal patches etc. If a company is involved in developing extended release tablets, the portfolio contains only extended release tablets in any therapeutic area and hence, the manufacturing facilities are created for extended release tablets.

Some companies may focus on therapeutic area(s) such as cardiovascular, metabolic disorders, oncology, immunology, etc. In this case the focus is on therapeutic area and hence, all types of dosage forms are developed in that particular therapeutic area(s).

Companies that focus on special population such as paediatrics, geriatrics, women health, etc., develop dosage forms suitable for the selected population. Many drug products developed for paediatrics and geriatrics who have swallowing difficulty are liquid orals, dispersible tablets, sachet for reconstitution, oral films etc.

Europe market always prefers blister packing while US market prefers bottle pack. Hence, the drug product designed should have stability in the packs based on geography.

CHAPTER 5

Design of Experiments for Formula and Process Optimization

Drug product development focus is to optimize the composition and process for manufacture of quality products. Scientists conduct various experiments to fulfil this main objective. The variables involved in composition are critical material attributes (CMAs) of API and excipients and the variable involved in process are the critical process parameters (CPPs) of each unit operation in the manufacturing of product. The more the number of variables involved in the experimentation, the number of experiments required to optimize the composition and process increases exponentially. The one factor at a time called OFAT approach is ineffective in cases where high number of variables are involved. OFAT approach is also called 'Edisonian' approach and the number of possible combination (experiments) increase exponentially as the number of factors increases. **Table 5.1** shows the number of experiments required based on factors and their levels. The number of levels of each variable to be studied further increases the number of experiments to be conducted in OFAT approach. Factors can influence the CQA either positively or negatively and hence, the interaction between factors happens for that CQA. For example, increased binder concentration increases the disintegration time (CQA) while disintegrant concentration increase reduces the disintegration time, hence, these two factors interact and the observed disintegration time is a net result of this interaction. Edosonian approach can't identify this interaction. The interpretation of results becomes cumbersome and scientist capabilities are critical in making decisions. Hence, a statistical tool is developed called Design of Experiments (DoE) that scientifically and statistically creates number of experiments based on number of factors and their levels. Design of Experiments (DOE) is a systematic and statistical approach for planning, conducting, and analysing controlled tests to understand how multiple input variables (factors) affect an output or response variable. Its core purpose is to determine which factors are most influential, optimize process settings, and achieve desired outcomes efficiently, saving time and resources compared to traditional one-factor-at-a-time experiments.

Table 5.1 Number of experiments by Edisonian Approach.

No of variables	5 levels	3 levels	2 levels
1	5	3	2
2	25	9	4
3	125	27	8
4	625	81	16
5	3125	243	32
10	9765625	59049	1024

5.1 Objective of Experiments

The objective of the experiments has to be defined very clearly so that proper design can be selected. The input variable or independent variable is called 'factor' and output or response is called 'dependent variable'. For example, quantity of dry binder is an input variable or factor and the hardness of tablet compressed at the same compression force is called response or dependent variable.

For example, the objective of experiment is to identify the sensitive factors of the proposed composition. The number of excipients in the composition are called 'factors' and different quantities of excipients to be studied are called 'levels' of the factor. Let us assume that the tablets are manufactured by dry blending of all components of composition followed by compression. Two unit operations are selected as important that is blending and compression to manufacture tablets. **Table 5.2** shows the proposed qualitative and quantitative composition of an immediate release tablet.

Table 5.2 Qualitative (Q1) and Quantitative (Q2) composition of Immediate Release Tablet.

S. No	Component	Functionality	Amount in mg
1	API*	Active ingredient	10
2	Microcrystalline cellulose	Diluent	100
3	Pregelatinized starch	Dry binder	15
4	Silicon dioxide	Glidant	2
5	Crospovidone	Disintegrant	4
6	Magnesium stearate	Lubricant	1.2
Total weight			132.2

*API PSD at two levels is considered D90 <10 & <30um

In order to optimize the composition quantitatively, two levels of excipients differing by 10% of proposed composition are considered. The process parameters of blending and compression are kept constant. Before proceeding to DoE experimentation, it is necessary to establish reproducibility of process by manufacturing the tablets with fixed composition and process parameters for each unit operation. This confirms that the experiments conducted with these fixed process parameters are suitable for assessing the impact of factor on critical quality attributes of tablet.

The next step is to list out the factors and their levels (amounts). **Table 5.3** lists the factors and levels. The lower level is represented by -1 and the higher level by +1 when the factor is studied at 2 levels and the midpoint is level '0'.

Table 5.3 Composition factors of an immediate release tablet.

S. No	Factor	Lower level	Central	Higher Level
1	API	PSD <10um	PSD <20um	PSD <30um
2	Microcrystalline cellulose	8.5	10	11.5
3	Pregelatinized starch	85	100	115
4	Silicon dioxide	12.75	15	17.25
5	Crospovidone	1.7	2	2.3
6	Magnesium stearate	3.4	4	4.6

Identification of Factor Variables

Factors can be divided into two types, continuous factors and categorical factors. Continuous factors are numerical variables that can be varied over a range, such as disintegrant quantity, fluid uptake or blender rotational speed. Categorical factors have qualitative attributes or levels that represent distinct categories, such as type of binder, type of flavour or type of blender or type of milling machine. For example, HPMC and HPC can be used in the composition to select best polymer.

In designing DoE experiments, the levels of factors are coded as -1 for lower level, +1 for higher level and '0' for central level. **Table 5.4** shows that conversion of levels in **Table 5.3** into coded levels.

Table 5.4 Coding of levels of factors for DoE.

S. No	Factor	Lower level	Central	Higher Level
1	API	-1	0	+1
2	Microcrystalline cellulose	-1	0	+1
3	Pregelatinized starch	-1	0	+1
4	Silicon dioxide	-1	0	+1
5	Crospovidone	-1	0	+1
6	Magnesium stearate	-1	0	+1

Identification of Response Variables

Response(s) or output to be measured for each experiments have to be identified which are generally the CQAs of product. In this example, the disintegration time, dissolution time for the release of 50%, 75% and 90% drug or dissolution profile can be the responses to be measured. Therefore, the response, target value and acceptance criteria have to be finalized to estimate the impact of the factors on responses **Table 5.5**.

Table 5.5 Responses, goal and acceptance criteria.

Responses		Goal	Acceptance ranges
1	Disintegration time	Minimum	NMT 3 minutes
2	Dissolution at 5min	Range	40-60
3	Dissolution at15min	Range	70-90
4	Dissolution at 30min	Range	NLT 85%

Selection of Correct Experimental Design

The selection of correct experimental design is a step by step process.

1. **Define research objective(s) or problem:** Define the acceptable outcome that is specific, measurable and meets the objective(s) or provides the solution to the problem.

   Factors to be evaluated (input variables) have to be identified and the low and high limits have to be decided. For example, disintegrant, binder, diluent and surfactant amounts are identified as input variables and the low and high amount for each excipient is defined.

   Responses to be measured (output variables) have to be identified and measured from the experimental data. For example, hardness, disintegration time and dissolution are identified as response variables and hence, they have to be measured for tablets resulted from each experiment.

   Control variables that have to be maintained constant during the experiment have to be identified and thoroughly controlled. For example, temperature and relative humidity are identified as control variables and hence, temperature is maintained at 25°C and relative humidity at 60%.

2. **Replication:** Repeating the same experiment multiple times. This repetition helps to quantify the natural variability in the data. This is to make sure that observed effects are consistent and not random. This is most important for the formulation scientist to perform any selected composition and process to determine whether the resultant dosage form

gives constant results with minimum acceptable variation or not. This confirmation is very critical before initiating time consuming, costly and labour intense full experimental design.

3. **Randomization:** Means to conduct experiments in a random order. This technique mitigates the impact of uncontrolled disturbance variables and reduces bias. It means there are some uncontrolled and unknown variables that may influence the response(s). For example, the experimental design resulted in a total of 10 experiments to be conducted for addressing the problem or meeting the objective(s). The order of execution of experiments should be randomized.
4. **Blocking:** It is used to control for the variability introduced by known but irrelevant variables. It involves grouping similar experimental units into blocks, and then randomizing treatments within these blocks. Blocking helps to isolate the effect of the primary factors of interest by accounting for the block-to-block variability. For example, the experimental objective is to compare the dissolution profile of marketed product and test product and four dissolution profiles for each product is planned. It is possible to conduct only four dissolutions per day. In such case, two blocks containing four dissolutions are made and in each block 2 marketed product and 2 test product are randomized for dissolution testing on first day and remaining four dissolution tests on 2nd day.

Design of Experiments

When many factors at different levels are involved in developing a formulation, then OFAT approach is not useful that need high number of experiments. In addition, the interpretation of results is also difficult because of possibility of interaction between factors and higher order interactions. Hence, statistical experimental designs called design of experiments are useful to optimize the formulation composition, manufacturing process or both. The quality by design guidance from regulatory authorities also recommend to use design of experiments in pharmaceutical development, manufacturing, quality control and quality assurance.

Two types of Design of experiments are used in pharmaceutical development.

1. Screening Designs
2. Optimization Designs

Screening Designs

The purpose of using screening designs is to identify significant factors that affect the CQAs and insignificant factors which may not impact CQAs so that they can be eliminated in subsequent DoE.

Major Advantages

Reduced number of experiments: Screening designs significantly reduce the number of experiments required to evaluate the factors compared with optimization designs.

Key factors: The analysis of the data enables identification of major factors affecting CQAs.

Efficient for large factor sets: The number of experiments is alarmingly high if optimized designs are used when number of factors and their levels are high.

Increased understanding: Even though the number of experiments is less, the statistical power of understanding the overall system still remains and reliable.

Disadvantages

Limited information on interactions: Factors may interact with each other with respect to a particular CQA and such information is limited in screening design. Two factors may interact synergistically or antagonistically.

Confounding of effects: The main effect of a factor is mixed with higher-order interactions making it difficult to isolate their individual effects.

Need for additional experiments: Because they screen out unimportant factors, a separate, more detailed experiment, like a full factorial design, is often needed to thoroughly analyse the significant factors.

The most commonly used screening designs are listed below.

1. Plackett-Burman design
2. Taguchi design
3. Fractional factorial design
4. Definitive Screening Design

Plackett-Burman design: This design is used to efficiently identify a few significant factors influencing a process or outcome from a larger set of potential variables. It requires fewer experimental runs than a full factorial design by testing factors at two levels (+1 and -1) and assuming that the effects of interactions between factors are negligible compared to the main effects. These designs are a cost-effective initial step to narrow down variables for subsequent optimization studies. Number of experiments required are based on the number of factors to be analysed. N-1 factors require N number of experiments. For example, 7 factors require 8 experiments. The design runs into multiples of 4 and hence, 5 or 6 or 7 factors use 8 experimental matrix of the Plackett-Burman **Table 5.6**.

Table 5.6 Plackett-Burman 8-run matrix.

Experiment Number	FACTORS						
	A	B	C	D	E	F	G
1	+	-	-	+	-	+	+
2	+	+	-	-	+	-	+
3	+	+	+	-	-	+	-
4	-	+	+	+	-	-	+
5	+	-	+	+	+	-	-
6	-	+	-	+	+	+	-
7	-	-	+	-	+	+	+
8	-	-	-	-	-	-	-

The factors (dependent or input variables) in the experiment and the response (independent or output variables) are correlated using a polynomial equation given below.

$$Y = A0 + A1X1 + A2X2 + A3X3 + \ldots\ldots + AnXn \qquad \ldots..(5.1)$$

Where Y is the response, A0 is the constant and A1 to An are the coefficients of the response values. Each response shall have a polynomial equation that correlates with the factors. The data is analysed using analysis of variance (ANOVA) and the probabilities of each factor effect are presented in the ANOVA table. In general, a $P<0.05$ is considered significant and those factors that have probability value of <0.05 are considered for further experimentation.

Taguchi Design: The experimental design proposed by Taguchi involves using orthogonal arrays to organize the parameters affecting the process and the levels at which they should be varied. Instead of having to test all possible combinations like the factorial design, the Taguchi method tests pairs of combinations. This allows for the collection of the necessary data to determine which factors most affect product quality with a minimum amount of experimentation, thus saving time and resources. The Taguchi arrays can be drawn out manually if factors and levels are less or large arrays can be derived from deterministic algorithms. Generally, arrays can be found online. The arrays are selected by the number of parameters (variables) and the number of levels (states).

Two-level designs include the L4, L8, and L16 matrices. The L4 design studies up to 3 factors. The most popular Taguchi designs are the L8 and L16 that study up to 7 and 15 factors respectively. **Table 5.7** provides L8 array of Taguchi design.

Table 5.7 Taguchi L8 array.

Experiment Number	Factor						
	A	B	C	D	E	F	G
1	1	1	1	1	1	1	1
2	1	1	1	2	2	2	2
3	1	2	2	1	1	2	2
4	1	2	2	2	2	1	1
5	2	1	2	1	2	1	2
6	2	1	2	2	1	2	1
7	2	2	1	1	2	2	1
8	2	2	1	2	1	1	2

Data analysis of Taguchi model provides an estimated regression coefficients table for each response characteristic selected. Use the p-values to determine which factors are statistically significant and use the coefficients to determine each factor's relative importance in the model. Relative magnitude of effect of each factor is considered in ranking them to give highest to lowest. This information is used to select most impactful factors for further studies and ignoring factors that have insignificant effect on the response(s).

Fractional Factorial Design: Full factorial design considers all possible experimental combination and hence, the number of experiments is high and become exorbitantly high number when the number of factors and their levels are more. Fractional factorial design considers strategic fraction of all possible experimental combinations to reduce experiments significantly while retaining the ability to identify main effect of factors.

In order to understand fractional factorial design, let us first understand full factorial design for three factors at two levels. The formula for estimating number of experiments for full factorial design is 2^k, where k is number of factors and 2 represents the levels of each factor. Hence, the number of experiments is 8. These 8 experiments represent, corners of a cube constructed with lower and higher level of each factor.

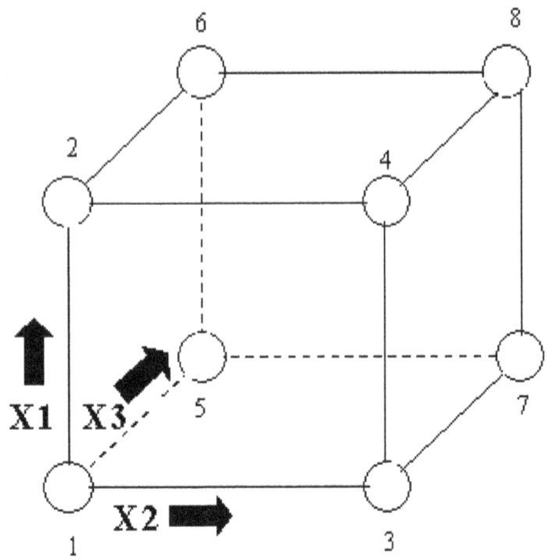

Figure 5.1 Full factorial design for 3 factors at 2 levels.

Fractional factorial design is nothing but reducing the number of experiments by creating a fraction of full factorial design. The formula for reducing experiments in fractional factorial design is 2^{k-1}. The number of experiments for 3 factors at 2 levels is 2^{3-1} is equal to 4. The full factorial design is halved and hence, ½ factorial design. Now the number of experiments to be conducted are only 4 and they are 1, 4, 6, & 7 or 2,3,5 and 8 in **Figure 5.1**. This process is applied for any number of factors at 2 level.

The full factorial design for 3 factors and 3 levels is 3^k and in this case, total number of experiments are 3^3=27. Fraction factorial design formula is 3^{k-1} and translates into 3^2=9 experiments.

Data analysis of fractional factorial designs involves estimating factor effects using regression, analysing Analysis of Variance (ANOVA) to identify significant variables, and using diagnostic plots like Pareto charts to visualize the effects.

Definitive Screening Design: "A Class of Three-Level Designs for Definitive Screening in the Presence of Second-Order Effects" is a 2011 Brumbaugh Award-winning paper by Bradley Jones and Christopher J. Nachtsheim that introduced Definitive Screening Designs (DSDs).

The factors effect on response (CQA) can be main effect, two-factor interaction and higher order interaction called quadratic effects. In addition, the main effect can be linear or non-linear. The disadvantage of screening designs explained above is their inability to identify interactions, quadratic effects, and non-linear effect of a factor. DSD needs experiments more than regular screening designs and significantly a smaller number of experiments than full factorial or optimization designs. For example, 8 factors at 2 level required 2^7 experiments as per full factorial design and the number of experiments is 256. The Plackett-Burman and Taguchi screening designs require 8 experiments while fraction factorial design requires 32 experiments with $1/8^{th}$ of full factorial design.

DSD design needs only 17 experiments for screening 8 factors. The distinctive features of DSD are:

1. Use of 3 levels of a factor at lower (-1), centre (0) and higher (+1)
2. Total number of experiments are double the number of factors (2X) plus centre level having all factors at '0'. Hence, for 8 factors, the number of experiments is 2*8=16 plus 1 (centre)= 17.
3. The runs of the design come in pairs that "mirror" each other. It means that the levels of factors in one run will have another run having exactly opposite level except for factor at centre level. For example,

Run 1	0	1	1	1	1	1	1	1
Run 2	0	-1	-1	-1	-1	-1	-1	-1

Therefore, DSD is capable of identifying main effect, two-factor interaction, and non-linearity of effect. The **Table 5.8** shows the DSD for 8 factors at 3 levels.

Table 5.8 Standard DSD design with one centre run.

Run	A	B	C	D	E	F	G	H
1	-1	-1	-1	-1	-1	-1	-1	-1
2	-1	-1	-1	1	1	1	1	-1
3	-1	-1	1	-1	1	1	-1	1
4	-1	-1	1	1	-1	-1	1	1
5	-1	1	-1	-1	1	-1	1	1
6	-1	1	-1	1	-1	1	-1	1
7	-1	1	1	-1	-1	1	1	-1
8	-1	1	1	1	1	-1	-1	-1
9	1	-1	-1	-1	-1	1	1	1
10	1	-1	-1	1	1	-1	-1	1
11	1	-1	1	-1	1	-1	1	-1
12	1	-1	1	1	-1	1	-1	-1
13	1	1	-1	-1	1	1	-1	-1
14	1	1	-1	1	-1	-1	1	-1
15	1	1	1	-1	-1	-1	-1	1
16	1	1	1	1	1	1	1	1
17	0	0	0	0	0	0	0	0

Data analysis in DSD is a step by step process. The first step is to identify the main effects of each factor and rank order the effects of each factor. The next step is to identify two factor interactions and finally to find out more complex interactions.

Pareto charts of effects is used to visualize the magnitude and statistical significance of all the effects. A reference line is provided in the chart that indicates cut-off for statistical significance to identify significant effects easily. The coefficient values for each factor is considered in understanding their contribution in the observed response. The higher the coefficient value the more significant is the factor. However, probability value <0.05 is considered significant.

The next step is to fit the data into a model and assess the goodness of fit. The best fit model provides the information about two factor interactions and the optimization of model fitting is used to identify higher level interactions. Residual plots validate the model assumptions by checking for non-random patterns. A normal probability plot of the residuals can check the normality of assumption in the model.

Hence, it can be seen that DSD provides more comprehensive analysis of data due to the design of experiments and gives all the important information to select the factors that influence the response(s) most.

Optimization Designs or Response Surface Methodology (RSM)

Once the screening design data is analysed for main effects, the important factors that impact the response(s) are considered for optimization while insignificant factors are ignored for further studies. The selected significant factors are input variables and the response(s) are out put variables. Design experiments are now used to optimize the selected factors and the designs used are called optimization designs. The composition or critical process parameters are optimized so that the drug product exhibits desired response(s). Response Surface Methodology (RSM) is a collection of mathematical and statistical techniques used to model, analyse, and optimize complex processes by finding the ideal conditions for a response variable. It involves design of experiments, execution of experiments as per plan, collection of data from the experiments on desired response(s) and then the data is fitted into a mathematical model that explains the observed data effectively. The most widely used designs for optimization of pharmaceutical composition and critical process parameters are central composite design (CCD), Box-Behnken design (BBD), standard mixture designs and optimal mixture designs. The significance of these designs is that the curvature of the response is also effectively captured using second order (quadratic) model. First order model is for linear response.

Central composite design (CCD): Central composite design is a combination of full or fractional factorial design + central point + axial points.

Factorial points are the corner points of the design space, representing the high and low levels of each factor (e.g., +1 and -1) while centre point is at the centre of design space and these can be included in full factorial or fraction factorial design but the important are axial points.

Axial Points (Star Points): These are points located along the axes, beyond the factorial points. They are set at levels of $+\alpha$ and $-\alpha$, where α is a value greater than 1, allowing for exploration of extreme values. The addition of axial points or also called star points specifically allows for the estimation of curvature, providing a more complete picture of the response surface than a simple factorial design. Each factor is studied at 5 levels.

The value of α is calculated using an equation $\alpha=(2^k)^{1/4}$. Where, k is the number of factorial runs. For 2 factors and 2 level full factorial the number of factorial runs is $2^k=4$ and the $\alpha= (2^2)^{1/4}= 1.414214$.

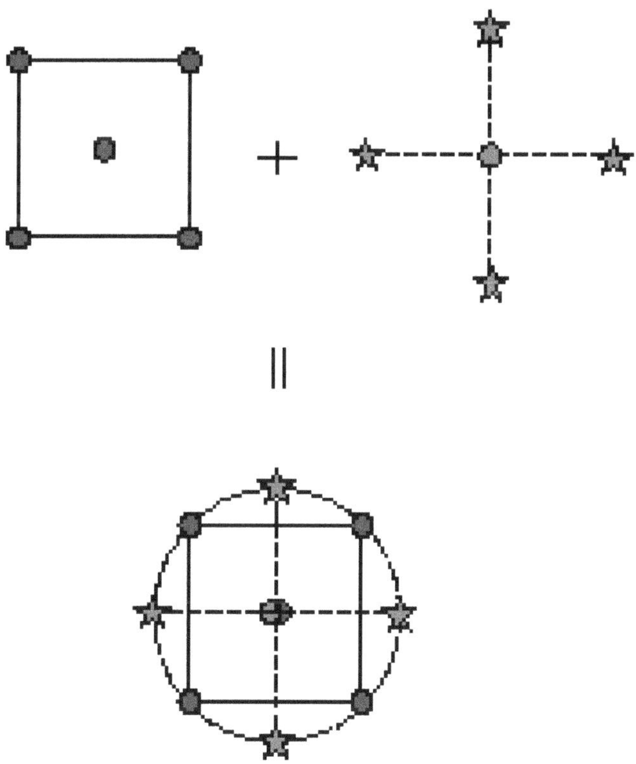

Figure 5.2 Formation of CCD from factorial design by adding axial points.

There are three variants in CCD based on the location of axial points in the design. They are circumscribed design (CCC), Inscribed design (CCI) and Face Centred design (CCF). **Figure 5.3** shows these variants.

CCDs are very efficient for fitting a second-order polynomial model, which can describe complex relationships and identify the optimal conditions for a process or system. The design is highly flexible and can be used with different types of factorial designs, including fractional factorial designs for efficiency. CCDs can be built up sequentially, starting with a factorial design and adding centre and axial points later as more information is gathered about the system **Figure 5.2**. **Figure 5.3.1** shows the formation of three types of design of CCD and **Figure 5.3.2** provides the process flow for using CCD effectively.

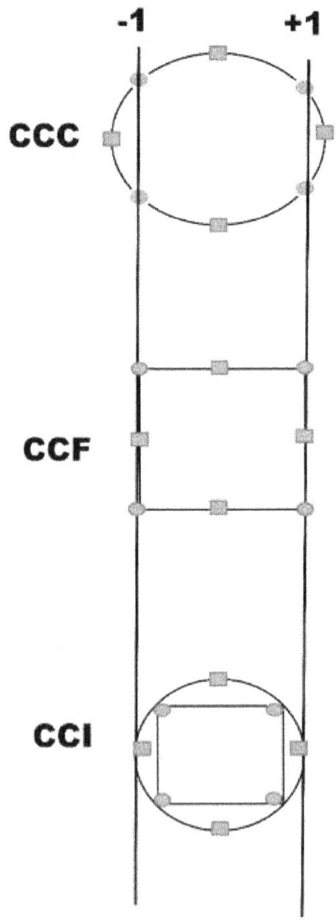

Figure 5.3.1 Three variants of CCD. Green points are different in each design and are axial points.

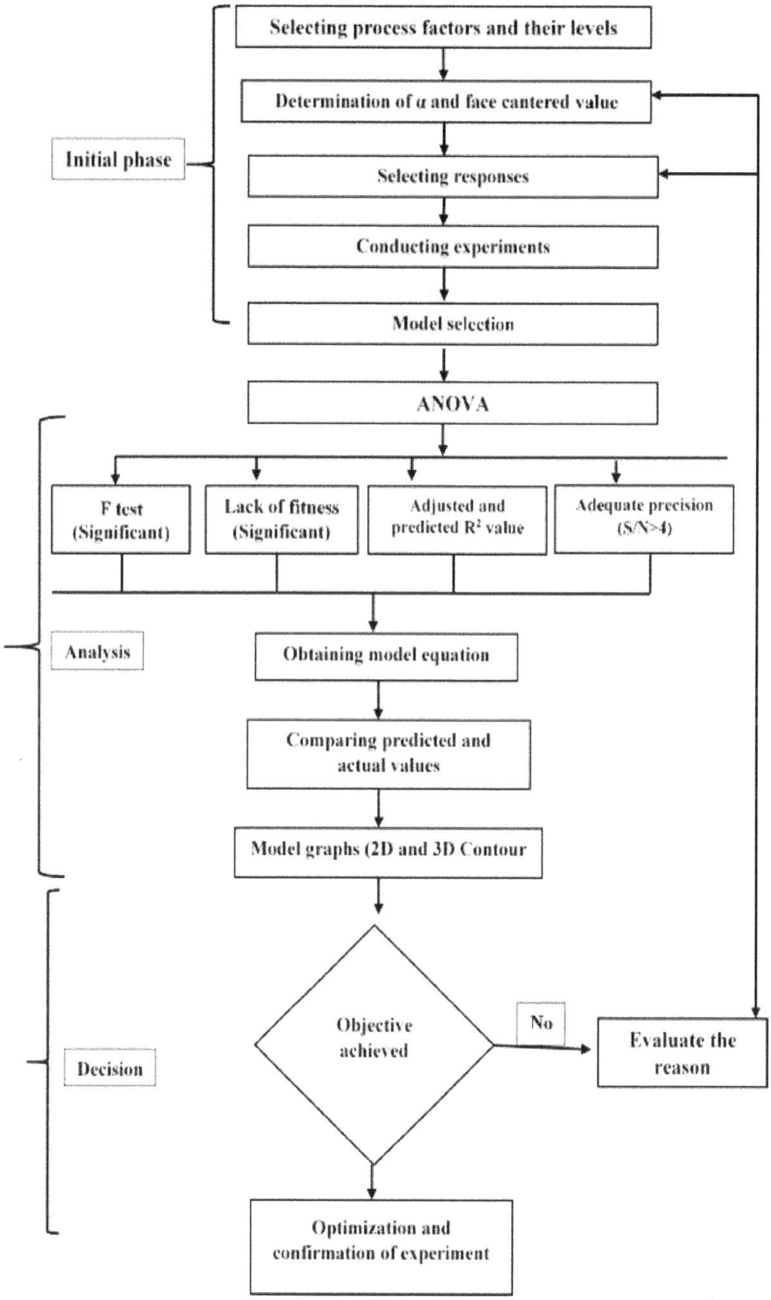

Figure 5.3.2 Process flow for CCD.

Box-Behnken Design (BBD):

- George E.P. Box and Donald Behnken have developed this design in 1960 for optimization of formula or process. It is more efficient than a full factorial design because it requires fewer experimental runs. BBD is a spherical, three-level design where factor settings are coded as low (-1), Centre (0), and high (+1). To design the BBD, simply the 2^k full factorial is used as the base design and then orthogonal blocks are created using the mid-levels for the other factors. This arrangement creates a "wire frame" structure inside the experimental space, avoiding extreme corner points where all factors are at their highest or lowest levels simultaneously. Central points are replicated runs with all factors at the centre level (0). These are included to estimate pure error and provide more precise estimates of coefficients near the centre of the design space. Therefore, it becomes a three-level factorial design, for which a full quadratic (second order) model can be fitted for the response surface **Figure 5.4**.

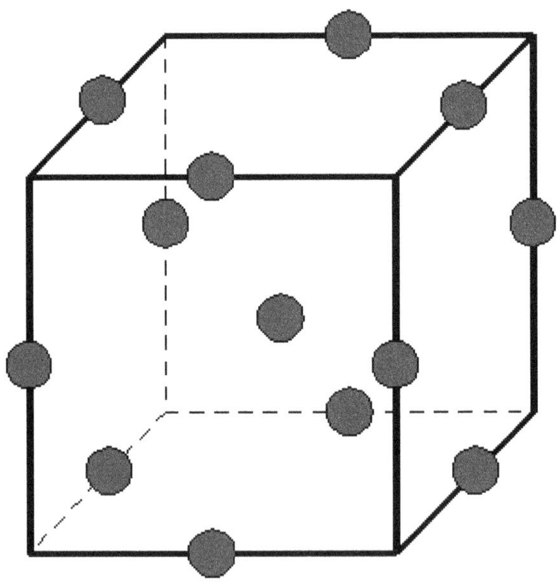

Figure 5.4 A Box-Behnken Design for Three Factors.

BBD requires fewer runs than a Central Composite Design (CCD) for the same number of factors. For example, a 3-factor BBD requires only 15 runs, whereas a full 3-level factorial design needs 27. The design is specifically constructed to fit a second-order polynomial (quadratic) model, which includes linear terms, two-factor interactions, and squared terms.

Table 5.9 shows the BBD for 3 and 4 factors and the number of experiments is 15 and 27 respectively. **Table 5.10** shows BBD for 5 factors and number of experiments is 46.

Table 5.9 Run order and standard order for 3 and 4 factors for BBD.

Run Order	Standard Order	X1	X2	X3
6	1	-1	-1	0
13	2	1	1	0
11	3	-1	-1	0
5	4	1	1	0
10	5	-1	0	-1
1	6	1	0	1
8	7	-1	0	-1
4	8	1	0	1
9	9	0	-1	-1
3	10	0	1	1
14	11	0	-1	-1
12	12	0	1	1
2	13	0	0	0
15	14	0	0	0
7	15	0	0	0

Run Order	Standard Order	X1	X2	X3	X4
6	1	-1	-1	0	0
3	2	1	-1	0	0
14	3	-1	1	0	0
19	4	1	1	0	0
8	5	0	0	-1	-1
2	6	0	0	1	-1
26	7	0	0	-1	1
20	8	0	0	1	1
4	9	-1	0	0	-1
21	10	1	0	0	-1
27	11	-1	0	0	1
10	12	1	0	0	1
11	13	0	-1	-1	0
13	14	0	1	-1	0
17	15	0	-1	1	0
25	16	0	1	1	0
5	17	-1	0	-1	0
16	18	1	0	-1	0
15	19	-1	0	1	0
9	20	1	0	1	0
24	21	0	-1	0	-1
23	22	0	1	0	-1
1	23	0	-1	0	1
22	24	0	1	0	1
18	25	0	0	0	0
7	26	0	0	0	0
12	27	0	0	0	0

Mixture Designs: In formulation development, the weight of the dosage form is fixed. For example, an immediate tablet weighting 250mg. When optimization experiments have to be conducted keeping weight as a constant but varying the drug and excipient means if one excipient is increased, then another excipients quantity has to be decreased so as to maintain constant weight of the tablet. Therefore, the sum of the percentages of all the components of the formulation is equal to 100%. In this situation, mixture design is more suitable for optimization of pharmaceutical drug product composition.

Table 5.10 Run order and standard order for 5 factors for BBD.

Run Order	Standard Order	X1	X2	X3	X4	X5
20	1	-1	-1	0	0	0
30	2	1	-1	0	0	0
40	3	-1	1	0	0	0
46	4	1	1	0	0	0
38	5	0	0	-1	-1	0
35	6	0	0	1	-1	0
37	7	0	0	-1	1	0
16	8	0	0	1	1	0
11	9	0	-1	0	0	-1
4	10	0	1	0	0	-1
13	11	0	-1	0	0	1
41	12	0	1	0	0	1
7	13	-1	0	-1	0	0
10	14	1	0	-1	0	0
12	15	-1	0	1	0	0
22	16	1	0	1	0	0
45	17	0	0	0	-1	-1
27	18	0	0	0	1	-1
32	19	0	0	0	-1	1
28	20	0	0	0	1	1
19	21	0	-1	-1	0	0
3	22	0	1	-1	0	0
8	23	0	-1	1	0	0
29	24	0	1	1	0	0
5	25	-1	0	0	-1	0
1	26	1	0	0	-1	0
17	27	-1	0	0	1	0
2	28	1	0	0	1	0
21	29	0	0	-1	0	-1
23	30	0	0	1	0	-1
14	31	0	0	-1	0	1
24	32	0	0	1	0	1
31	33	-1	0	0	0	-1
9	34	1	0	0	0	-1
25	35	-1	0	0	0	1
36	36	1	0	0	0	1
42	37	0	-1	0	-1	0
26	38	0	1	0	-1	0
6	39	0	-1	0	1	0
43	40	0	1	0	1	0
39	41	0	0	0	0	0
44	42	0	0	0	0	0
15	43	0	0	0	0	0
34	44	0	0	0	0	0
33	45	0	0	0	0	0
18	46	0	0	0	0	0

When the mixture components are subject to the constraint that they must sum to 100% or unity, there are standard mixture designs for fitting standard models, such as *Simplex-Lattice* designs and *Simplex-Centroid* designs. When mixture components are subject to additional constraints, such as a maximum/minimum value for each component, designs other than the standard mixture designs, called constrained mixture designs or *Extreme-Vertices* designs, are appropriate.

Simplex-Lattice Design: The design points form a grid-like structure (a lattice) on the simplex, ensuring even coverage of the possible mixture combinations. The degree of the design, m, determines the possible levels for each component's proportion. A simplex-lattice mixture design of degree m consists of m+1 points of equally spaced values between 0 and 1 for each component. If m = 2 then possible fractions are 0, 1/2, 1. For m = 3 the possible levels are 0, 1/3, 2/3, 1. m does not take the value of one (1) because all other designs will always have to contain it. When $m = 1$, this represents single-mixture experiment.

When m=2, the {3,2} matrix is considered and the factor values take 0, 0.5, and 1. **Figure 5.5** shows the experimental design.

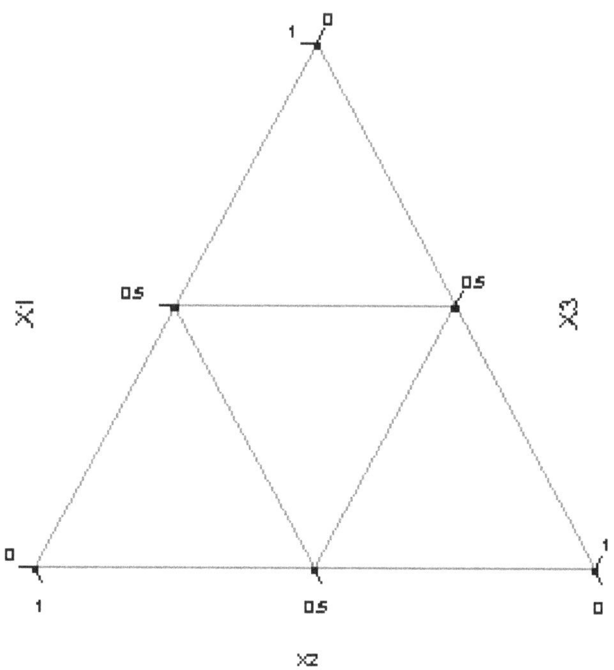

Figure 5.5 Simplex-Lattice design for 3 factors and 2 degrees of design.

Let us consider q factors and m degree of the design the matrix is represented by $\{q, m\}$. If the number of factors are 3 and degree of design is 3 then the matric {3, 3} has to be constructed. The number of points are m+1=3+1 = 4 i.e., 0, 1/333, 1.667 and 1. The factors are represented by X1, X2, X3. The simplex-lattice is presented in **Figure: 5.6**. The number of experiments to be performed, Xi, is calculated using the equation, Xi= 0, 1/m, 2/m, 3/m…,1 , q and all possible combinations (mixtures) of the proportions from this equation are used.

Number of experiments for {3, 3} matrix is 10 and the experimental compositions of factors is presented in the **Figure 5.6**. It can be observed from the experiments that 3 experiments contain pure factor, 6 binary mixtures and one ternary mixture **Table 5.11**.

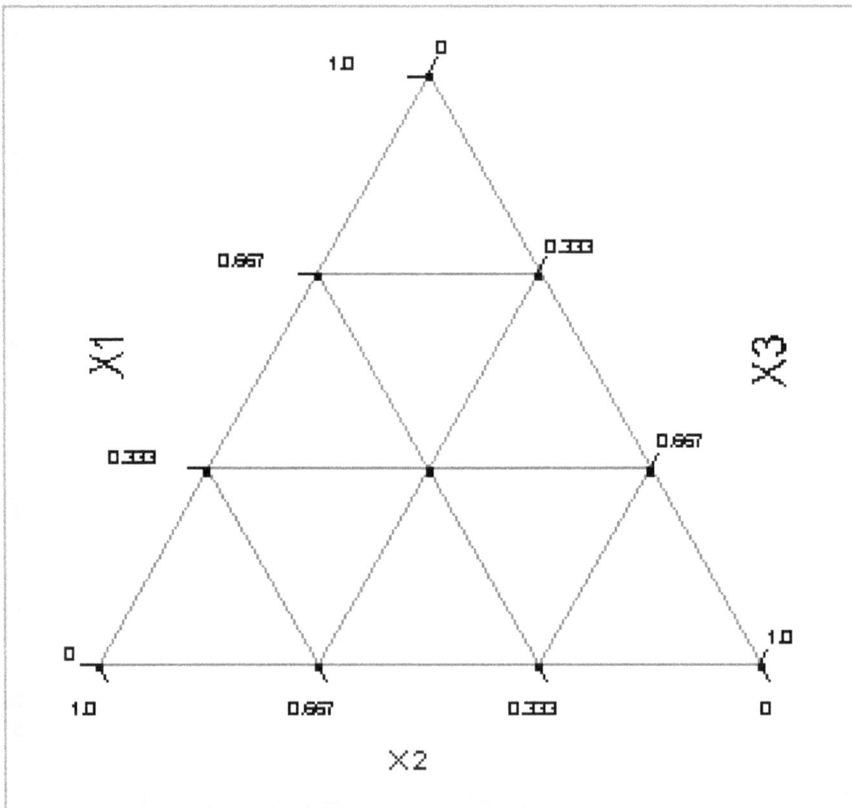

Figure 5.6 Simplex-Lattice design for 3 factors and 3 degrees of design.

Table 5.11 Simplex Lattice Design.

X_1	X_2	X_3
0	0	1
0	0.333	0.667
0	0.667	0.333
0	1	0
0.333	0	0.667
0.333	0.333	0.333
0.333	0.6667	0
0.667	0	0.333
0.667	0.333	0
1	0	0

Simplex-Centroid Design

Simplex centroid design considers experimental points in the centre of the factor values also. In the *q*-component simplex-centroid design, the number of distinct points is $2^q - 1$. The experiments contain:

- Pure Components: The vertices of the simplex, representing 100% of a single component (e.g., (1,0,0...0)).
- Binary Mixtures: All possible mixtures of two components in equal proportions (e.g., (1/2, 1/2, 0...0)).
- Tertiary Mixtures: All mixtures of three components in equal proportions (e.g., (1/3, 1/3, 1/3, 0...0)), and so on.
- Overall Centroid: The mixture where all q components are present in equal proportions (1/q, 1/q, ... 1/q).

The simple centroid for 3 factors requires $2^3-1=7$ experiments. The design can be augmented by including 3 more experiments as depicted in **Figure 5.7**. Repetition of central experiments more than one time is also practiced by scientists. **Figure 5.8** shows the repetition of centre experiment three times leading to a total of 12 experiments.

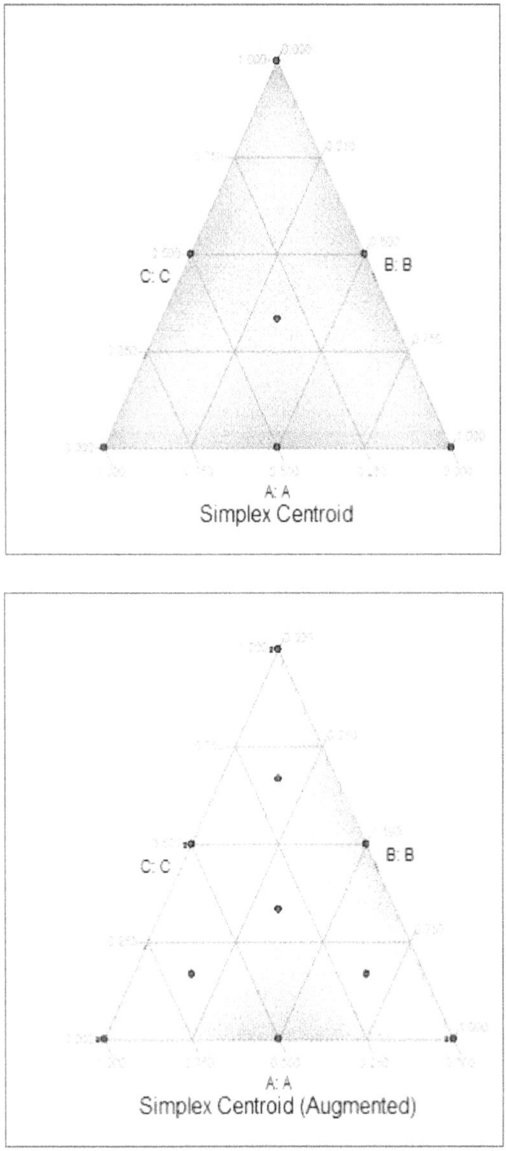

Figure 5.7 Simplex Centroid and Simplex Centroid Augmented designs.

Let us consider an experiment consisting of 3 solvents (factors) for solubilisation of a poorly soluble drug. Water, ethanol and acetone are miscible solvents and the experiments are conducted with three solvents to get maximum solubility of drug. The experimental design used was a simplex centroid with augmentation and repetition of centre point thrice.

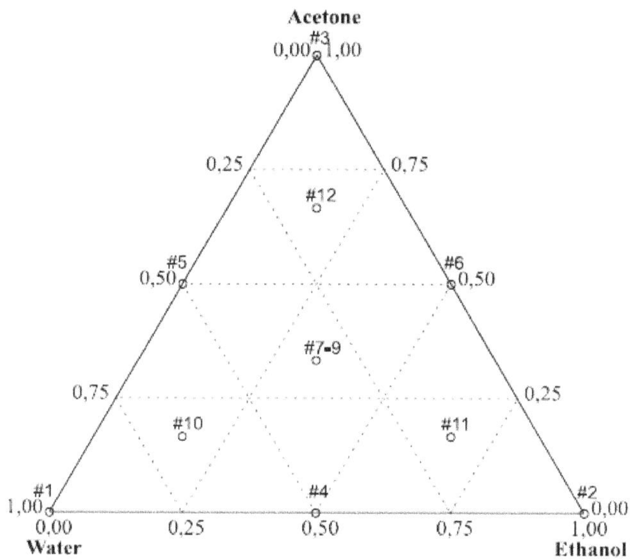

Figure 5.8 Simplex centroid design with augmentation and repetition of centre experiments 3 times.

Extreme-Vertices Design

Extreme vertices designs are mixture designs that cover only a sub-portion or smaller space within the simplex. These designs must be used when chosen design space is not a simplex-lattice design. The presence of both lower and upper bound constraints on the components often create this condition. **Table 5.12** shows the constraints on factors and hence, the design is extreme vertices (**Figure 5.9**).

Table 5.12 Limits of each factor.

Factor	Limits	
X1	0.05	0.25
X2	0.1	0.3
X3	0.1	0.3
X4	0.1	0.4
X5	0	1

The extreme vertices design is presented in the pictorial form in **Figure 5.9**.

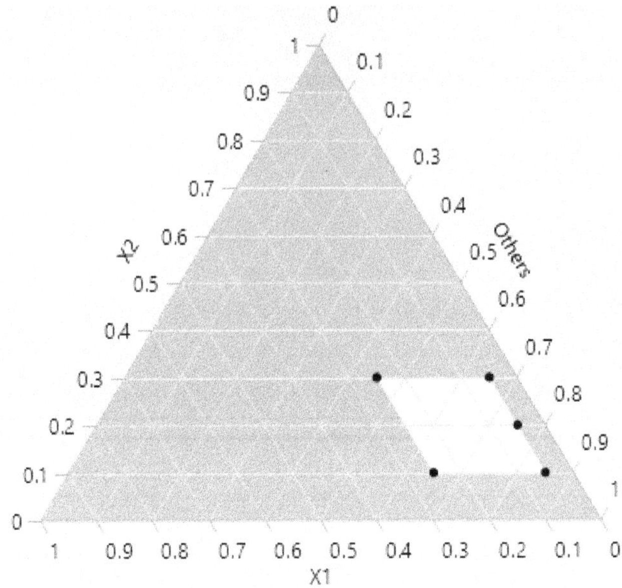

Figure 5.9 Extreme-Vertices Design.

It should be noted that two factors, X1 &X2 having limits are considered and other factors are considered together to create ternary diagram. Similar ternary diagrams can be prepared by selecting two factors and all others as one factor. The intent of the design is to consider the limits and optimize the composition within the prescribed limits.

Optimal Mixture Designs

Optimal design also known as custom design is used when standard designs can't accommodate additional requirements or adjustments for the composition or process. Some of the situation under which optimal designs are preferred are listed below.

1. The difference between the high and low of all the mixture components not the same.
2. Inclusion of constraints other than the factor limits
3. Inclusion of mixture and process variable in the same design
4. Studying two independent mixtures in the same design
5. To reduce the experimental runs compared with standard designs
6. Inclusion of replication uniformly throughout the design

Optimal designs are categorized as D-optimal, A-optimal, I-optimal and G-optimal based on the objective to be achieved from the data. These are custom-built and more flexible, allowing for irregular experimental regions and a smaller number of runs. It should be noted that optimal designs are used only when the user requirements are not addressed by the standard designs. The basic information available from each category of optimal design is presented here.

D-optimal designs: A D-optimal design is an experimental design criterion focused on minimizing the *generalized variance of the parameter estimators.* It is particularly useful for complex experimental regions, non-standard models, or when classical experimental designs are too large or impractical, and it uses an iterative search algorithm to select the best experimental runs from a candidate set.

A-optimal designs: The focus in this design is to minimize the *average variance of the parameter estimators.*

I-optimal designs: An I-optimal design is an experimental design criterion focused on minimizing *the average variance of prediction* across the entire experimental design space, making it ideal for tasks like optimizing process parameters or predicting outcomes.

G-optimal designs: *G*-optimal designs are those which minimize the worst-case prediction variance. Thus, such designs are of interest if prediction is a primary component of the post-experiment analysis and decision making. It minimizes the *maximum variance of the predicted values.*

V-optimal designs: V-optimal design in experimental design minimizes the *average variance of predicted regression responses* over the experimental region. This design is used to achieve a desired level of precision for predictions at pre-specified points.

Conduct of experiments and data collection

Once the experimental design is completed, standard order runs are randomized to get execution order of experiments called run order. The experiments have to be conducted in the recommended order, control variables should be maintained constant where applicable, and responses for each experiment have to be measured with sensitive equipment. The data should be collected as per the experimental design where the design provides columns for entering the response.

For example, the experiments are designed for the optimization of composition of immediate release tablets. The entire process followed during the execution of experiment, the weights of each ingredient, the percent yield at each process step and the final yield have to be recorded as per GLP. The tablets produced from each experiment have to be evaluated for the defined responses such as hardness, disintegration time, dissolution etc. The units of measurement of a response should be same across all the experiment to avoid confusion and wrong results. All the responses have to be properly filled in the experimental design and kept ready for analysis using appropriate software.

Analysis of Data and Modelling

The purpose of data analysis is to identify patterns, trends, and relationships in data to understand valuable information and use for decision making. This involves reviewing data, correcting errors (cleansing) and converting data to a usable format (transformation). The techniques used in data analysis are based on relevant questions about data such as what happened (descriptive), why it happened (diagnostic), what might happen (predictive), and what should be done (prescriptive). The data is presented as tables, figures, charts and three-dimensional plots etc., to clearly understand the summary of findings.

Modelling involves creating a mathematical representation of the relationship between input factors and output responses of a system to understand, predict, and optimize its behaviour. It is used to provide a precise mathematical equation(s) that describe the observed data and to show the effect of each factor on response(s) and relation between them. The data can be described either by linear models or nonlinear models depending on the relationship between factors and responses. Linear regression models data with a straight-line relationship, assuming the relationship between variables is constant and additive. Nonlinear regression fits data to a predefined curve when the relationship is curved, such as exponential or sigmoid. Complex relationship between factor and response may require polynomial regression to describe the observed data.

Prediction Capability of a Model

The very purpose of conducting experiments using statistical design of experiments is not only to understand the relationship between the factors and observed responses but to predict the composition or critical process parameters that would provide desired properties. Prediction capability of a model is its ability to forecast the responses when factors are changed or to provide specific levels of each factor that would result in desired response(s). For example, modelling of dissolution data of immediate release tablet is established and now the formulator desires a particular dissolution profile from the tablet, then the model should be capable of providing the suitable composition or critical process parameters to achieve the desired dissolution profile. Or when a new composition is proposed, the expected dissolution profile has to be generated by the model. This capability is assessed by how well the model performs on new, unseen data, its generalizability to related situations, and its accuracy in identifying patterns to provide actionable insights for decision-making and resource allocation.

CHAPTER 6

Design Space

6.1 Design Space

The design of experiments from screening to response surface methodology are meant for identifying and optimizing critical material attributes (CMAs) and critical process parameters (CPPs) that impact critical quality attributes (CQAs) of drug product. Each factor (CMA or CPP) may have influence on different CQA and in order to meet all CQAs of drug product, there is a need to finalize the acceptable ranges of each CMA and CPP so that the drug product is manufactured within these specified ranges would always produce a product with defined CQAs.

A design space is defined as the multidimensional region of input variables (like process parameters and material attributes) that have been shown to consistently deliver a product meeting its quality requirements. Working within the established design space is considered normal process operation and is not a regulatory change, while operating outside it is a change that requires further review.

The step by step process in building design space for the manufacture of drug product is discussed here.

1. Identify CMAs, CPPs and CQAs for the manufacture of drug product.
2. Use screening design when the factors are high in number to reduce the number of experiments to be conducted. Identify the significant factors influencing the CQAs of the product.
3. Select the appropriate response surface methodology design to study the significant CMAs and CPPs effect on CQAs.
4. Conduct the experiment as per the design layout and collect the response(s) using best analytical methods and document the details.
5. Analyse the data obtained from the experiments using various statistical tools, graphs and mathematical models. Construct the counter plots for all CMAs and CPPs with selected response(s).
6. Overlay the graphs to identify the space within which the CQAs are meeting the specifications. This space is called "design Space".

7. Prediction is the ability of design space and hence, it is possible to define CQAs and predict the CMAs and CPPs required to be used. In addition, the CMAs and CPPs can be fixed within design space and CQAs can be predicted. Hence, Validate the design space by conducting experiments within the design space.
8. Implement control strategy by designing a system to monitor and control the input variables within the design space throughout the manufacturing process.

6.2 Initiation of Pharmaceutical Product Development using QbD

The beginning of pharmaceutical development starts with defining QTPP and identification of CMAs, CPPs, CQAs and control variables. The risk assessment is the next step to list out factors (CMAs and CPPs) that may impact the CQAs of the product. Once the factors are identified the target level for each factor has to be decided based on prior knowledge, experience and literature. The lower and upper limits of each factor have to be finalized for studying their influence on CQAs. Formulation scientist has to optimize both the composition and each unit operation involved in the manufacturing of dosage form. Let us consider a case study to understand the application of design of experiments in creating design space.

A BCS class II drug has to be formulated as an immediate release tablet using direct compression method. The qualitative composition of the tablet is finalized with prior knowledge and literature review and the following qualitative composition is finalized after risk assessment as detailed in previous chapters. The composition, functionality, amount, CMA and ranges of CMA are presented in **Table 6.1**.

Table 6.1

S. No	Component	Functionality	Target Quantity in mg	CMA	Low and high levels of CMA
1	API	Therapeutic agent	10	PSD	10um and 30um
2	Microcrystalline cellulose (MCC)	Insoluble diluent	50	Quantity	30 and 70
3	Lactose monohydrate	Soluble diluent	50	Quantity	30 and 70

Table 6.1 *Contd...*

S. No	Component	Functionality	Target Quantity in mg	CMA	Low and high levels of CMA
4	Croscarmellose sodium	Disintegrant	5	Quantity	3 and 7
5	Talc	Glidant	2	Quantity	1 and 3
6	Magnesium stearate	Lubricant	1	Quantity	0.5 and 1.5
	Total weight of tablet		118		

Process feasibility: The next step is to study the process feasibility using target composition. In this step, the process flow and target CPPs are fixed to manufacture a prototype immediate release tablet. The process flow for the manufacture of immediate release tablets is presented in **Figure 6.1**. The purpose of process feasibility study is not to get a tablet with desired qualities but to establish that tablets can be manufactured with the process using fixed CPPs. It has been observed that the blend is flowing properly and the blend was compressed into tablet.

Reproducibility: Once the process feasibility is established, the next step is to check the reproducibility of process to prove that the process is robust. It should be noted that the objective is to check some CQAs that give confidence that the process is robust and produce tablets with reproducible CQAs but not to compare with desired specification of CQAs. In this example, hardness variation, weight variation, disintegration time and dissolution of tablets produced two times are compared. This verification is critical for optimization of composition using fixed CPPs. The process is optimized using optimized composition. However, it is possible to combine both composition variables (CMAs) and process variables (CPPs) to have single design of experiments but the number of factors shall be high demanding for high number of experiments. Hence, composition is finalized first followed by process.

Screening design: A full factorial design to study 6 factors at 2 levels requires 64 experiments. The resources and time required to execute 64 experiments is very high and it is unknown whether all the factors significantly impact the CQAs or not. Therefore, screening design is used to identify by most significant CMAs that impact CQAs. The number of experiments required for screening using Plackett-Burman are N for N-1 factors. In this case, the number of factors is 6 and hence, the number of experiments is 7. However, Plackett-Burman experimental design is multiple of 4 experiments, therefore, 8 experimental design with one dummy factor is possible but 12 experiments are considered that would provide more insight into the data including interactions. **Table 6.2** provides the screening design of Plackett-Burman.

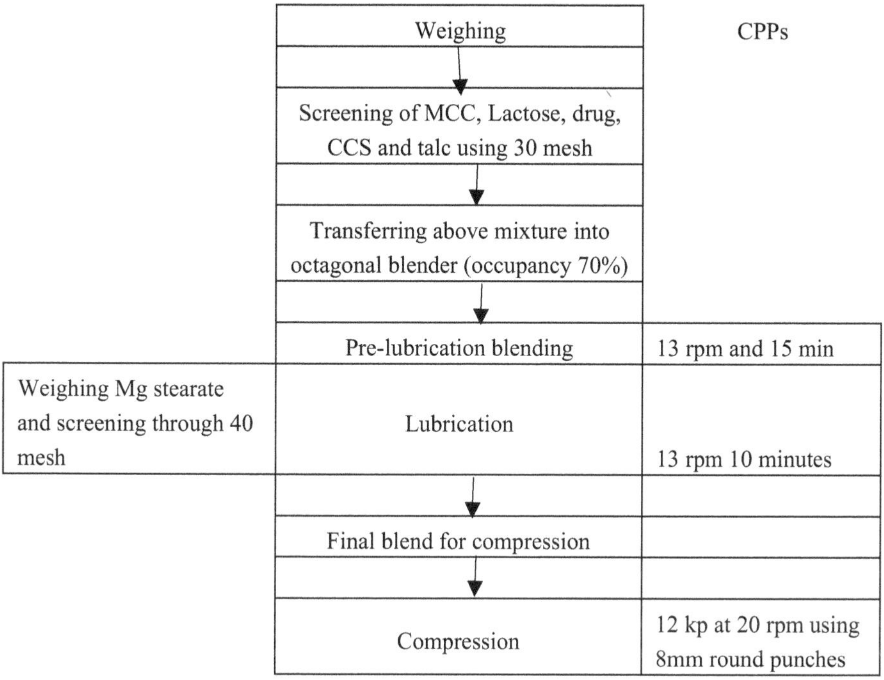

Figure 6.1 Process flow for the manufacture of immediate release tablets.

Software packages useful in designing and analysing design of experiments are available commercially and from open source. Since, the data analysis is rigorous and laborious, it is always advisable to use proper software for DoE.

Comprehensive, user friendly and commercial software are Minitab, JMP and Design Expert.

Open source software with programming options are R, Python and JASP.

Minitab® software is used for this example.

The experiments are conducted as per the design given in **Table 6.2** and the responses are recorded for each experiment. Various options are available to analyse the data obtained from the experiment. **Figures 6.2** (A, B &C) shows the main effect of each factor on responses (DT, Dissolution at 15 min and dissolution at 30 min).

Table 6.2 Plackett-Burman design to screen 6 factors at 2 levels.

StdOrder	RunOrder	PtType	Blocks	PSD	MCC	Lactose	CCS	Talc	Mg. Searate	DT min	Disso 15 min	Disso 30 min
4	1	1	1	30	30	70	7	1	1.5	5	30	65
5	2	1	1	30	70	30	7	3	0.5	3	35	70
2	3	1	1	30	70	30	7	1	0.5	3	38	73
3	4	1	1	10	70	70	3	3	0.5	5	42	75
7	5	1	1	10	70	70	7	1	1.5	3.5	46	80
9	6	1	1	10	30	30	7	3	1.5	5	47	82
11	7	1	1	10	70	30	3	1	1.5	6	45	80
12	8	1	1	10	30	30	3	1	0.5	8	36	74
10	9	1	1	30	30	30	3	3	1.5	8	28	62
6	10	1	1	30	70	70	3	3	1.5	7	26	60
1	11	1	1	30	30	70	3	1	0.5	9	24	58
8	12	1	1	10	30	70	7	3	0.5	8	28	60

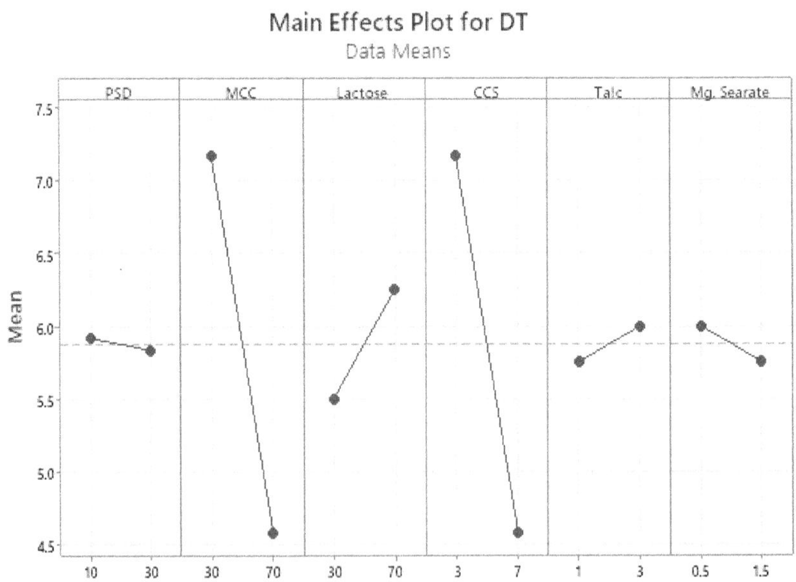

A

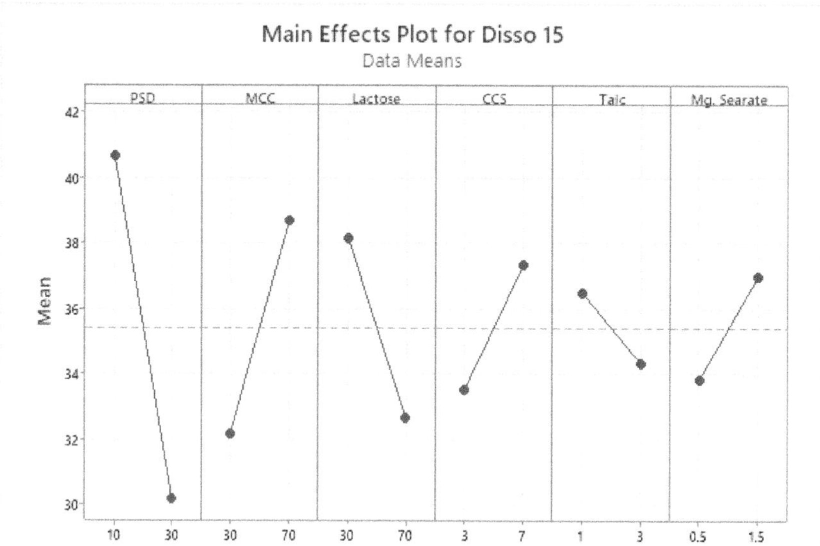

B

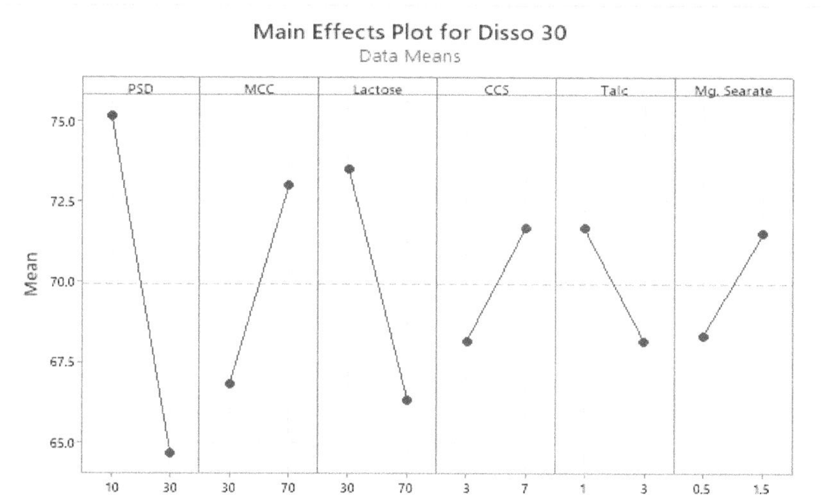

C

Figure 6.2 A- Main effect of factors on DT, B- Main effect of factors on dissolution at 15 min and C- Main effect of factors on dissolution at 30 min. The summary of effect of each factor on response is given in **Table 6.3**.

Table 6.3 Summary of main effect of each factor.

Factor	Main effect on Responses		
	Disintegration time	**Dissolution at 15 min**	**Dissolution at 30 min**
API PSD	Has no significant effect	Higher the particle size the lower the dissolution	Higher the particle size the lower the dissolution
MCC	Higher amount decreased DT	Higher amount increased dissolution	Higher amount increased dissolution
Lactose	Has no significant effect	Higher amount decreased dissolution	Higher amount decreased dissolution
CCS	Higher amount decreased DT	Higher amount increased dissolution	Higher amount increased dissolution
Talc	No significant effect	No significant effect	No significant effect
Magnesium stearate	No significant effect	No significant effect	No significant effect

Interpretation: Disintegration time is always in acceptable limits. Dissolution rate can be increased using low particle size API, relatively high amount of MCC and low amount of Lactose and high amount of CCS. Talc and magnesium have no significant impact on the responses studied.

The data can also be analysed for interactions between factors. **Figure 6.3 (A, B & C)** provide the details of interactions between factors for each response.

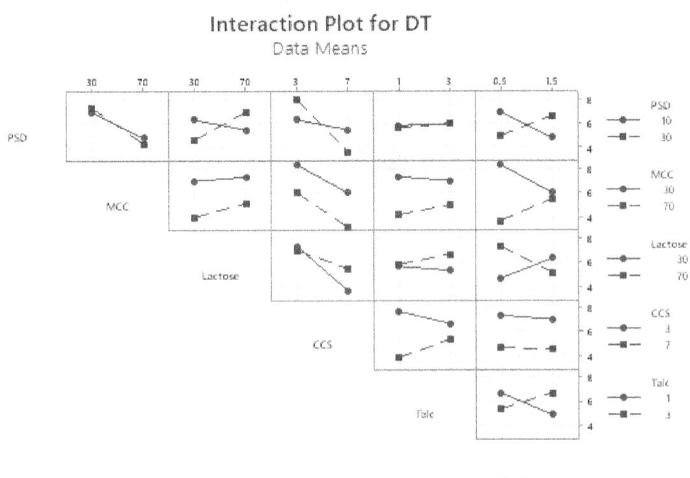

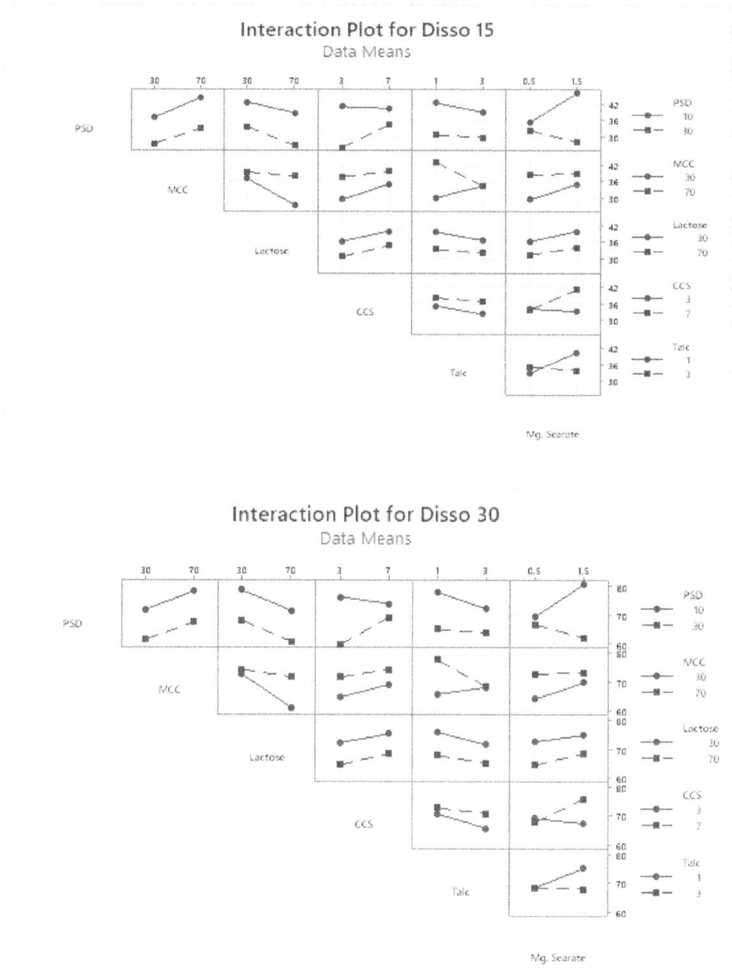

Figure 6.3 A- Interaction plot for DT, B- interaction plot for dissolution at 15 min and C- interaction plot for dissolution at 30 min.

The plot to be read against two factors and if two lines are crossed then an interaction is suspected. For example, in interaction plot of DT, PSD of API is showing interaction with Lactose, CCS and Magnesium stearate. Magnesium stearate is showing interaction with lactose and Talc.

There is no significant interaction for dissolution at 15 and 30 min.

Counter plots: Counter plots of two factors for a selected response would help the formulator to see the effect of the ratios of these two factors on the selected response. The number of counter plots would be high to present here but MCC and Lactose counter plot is selected for explaining the use of these plots (**Figure 6.4**).

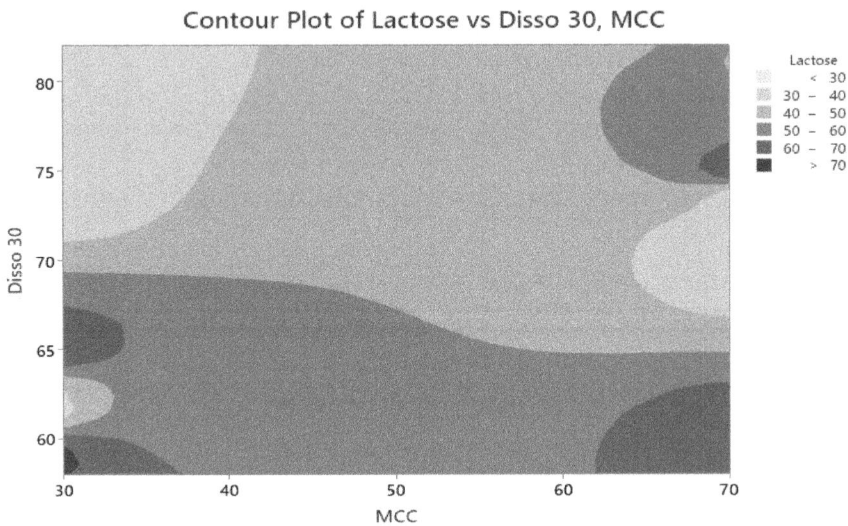

Figure 6.4 A counter plot of MCC and Lactose for dissolution at 30 min.

It is possible to maximize the dissolution at 30 minutes by selecting the optimum ratio of MCC and lactose from the counter plot.

Conclusions:

1. API PSD, MCC, Lactose and CCS have shown significant effect on selected CQAs. These factors have to be further studied to optimize their amounts.
2. Talc and Magnesium stearate have no significant effect on selected CQAs.

Optimization Designs

Response Surface Methodology (RSM) is used for the optimization of the factors. Discussion on different types of designs are discussed in the previous chapter. Since, pharmaceutical composition has to be finalized, a mixture design is more suitable for current example. Simplex centroid design is selected with four significant factors with lower and upper levels similar to those used in screening design (**Table 6.2**). Minitab® software is used to generate the experiments and all the experiments were conducted as per the run order and the responses are recorded in **Table 6.4**.

Table 6.4 Simplex Centroid design for the optimization of 4 factors.

StdOrder	RunOrder	PtType	Blocks	PSD	MCC	Lactose	CCS	DT	Disso 15	Disso 30
28	1	0	1	20	50	50	5	5	28	81
10	2	1	1	30	30	30	7	5.5	25	80
4	3	1	1	30	70	30	3	5	24	75
11	4	1	1	10	70	30	7	3.5	35	89
2	5	1	1	30	30	30	3	6.5	22	70.4
6	6	1	1	30	30	70	3	8.5	19	60.8
30	7	0	1	20	50	50	5	5.1	26	83.2
20	8	-1	1	20	90	50	5	4.5	29	92.8
18	9	-1	1	40	50	50	5	5	27	86.4
26	10	0	1	20	50	50	5	5	28	89.6
17	11	-1	1	0	50	50	5	5	0	0
8	12	1	1	30	70	70	3	6.5	22	70.4
13	13	1	1	10	30	70	7	5.5	20	64
31	14	0	1	20	50	50	5	5	29	92.8
7	15	1	1	10	70	70	3	6	21	67.2
21	16	-1	1	20	50	10	5	4	29	92.8
5	17	1	1	10	30	70	3	6	20	64
27	18	0	1	20	50	50	5	5	29	92.8
12	19	1	1	30	70	30	7	4	26	83.2
24	20	-1	1	20	50	50	9	3.5	32	92
25	21	0	1	20	50	50	5	5.1	36	95
15	22	1	1	10	70	70	7	5	28	89.6
3	23	1	1	10	70	30	3	6	22	70.4
29	24	0	1	20	50	50	5	5	28	89.6
23	25	-1	1	20	50	50	1	9	18	57.6
22	26	-1	1	20	50	90	5	8	19	60.8
9	27	1	1	10	30	30	7	5.5	22	70.4
16	28	1	1	30	70	70	7	5.3	24	76.8
14	29	1	1	30	30	70	7	8	20	64
19	30	-1	1	20	10	50	5	8	19	60.8
1	31	1	1	10	30	30	3	9	18	57.6

Data Analysis: Several options are available in software to generate useful equations, graphs and counter plots to understand the effect of each factor on the CQAs (responses). In the current example, DT, dissolution at 15min and 30 minutes are considered as CQAs. Any number of CQAs can be included in responses.

The first step is to fit the data into an equation that describes the observed CQAs. Hence, regression analysis of data is carried out to generate equations for each CQA.

Regression Equation for DT

DT = 8.488 + 0.0117 PSD - 0.04208 MCC + 0.02875 Lactose - 0.4625 CCS

In order check the goodness of fit of the regression equation an ANOVA is carried out.

Regression Equation for Dissolution at 15 minutes is

Disso at 15 min = 11.95 + 0.208 PSD + 0.1167 MCC - 0.0833 Lactose + 1.250 CCS

Regression Equation for Dissolution at 30 minutes is

Disso at 30 min = 38.8 + 0.755 PSD + 0.322 MCC - 0.215 Lactose + 3.13 CCS

Let us observe the regression equations for dissolution at 15 and 30 min. Lactose is having negative effect on dissolution while other factors have positive effect. The relative value of coefficients of the factors indicate their significance on the CQA (response). As expected disintegrant, CCS, has highest impact on dissolution followed by PSD and MCC. It gives clear direction to the formulator to optimize the composition to increase dissolution of tablets and the prediction can be made using the regression equations. If dissolution data is generated for several time points, then regression equation for each time point can be used to predict complete dissolution profile of proposed compositions. This is the importance DoE than OFAT approach.

Interaction Plot: Interaction plots for each response (CQA) are used to understand the interaction between factors. For example, an interaction plot for dissolution at 15 min is presented in **Figure: 6.5**.

It is evident from the plot that there are no significant interactions between factors studied for dissolution at 15 min.

Probability Plot: Probability plot of each factor can be generated to get 95% confidence interval for observed CQA. This gives the random variation observed in CQA from a factor at a given level and provides 95%CI limits. **Figure 6.6** shows the probability plot for CCS.

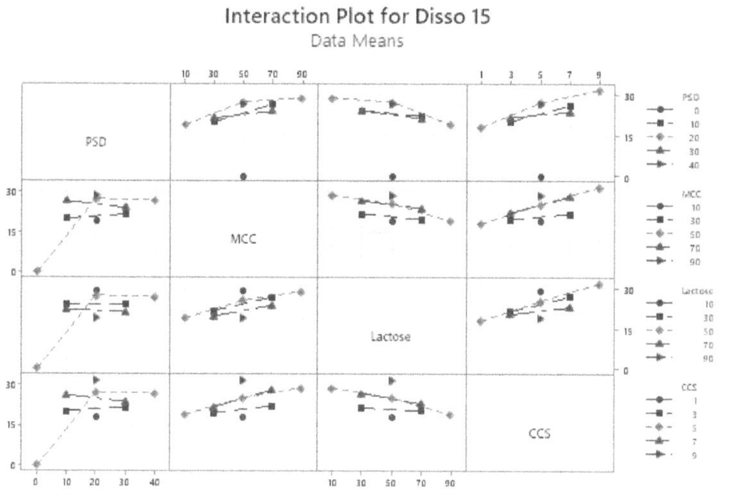

Figure 6.5 Interaction plot for dissolution at 15 minutes.

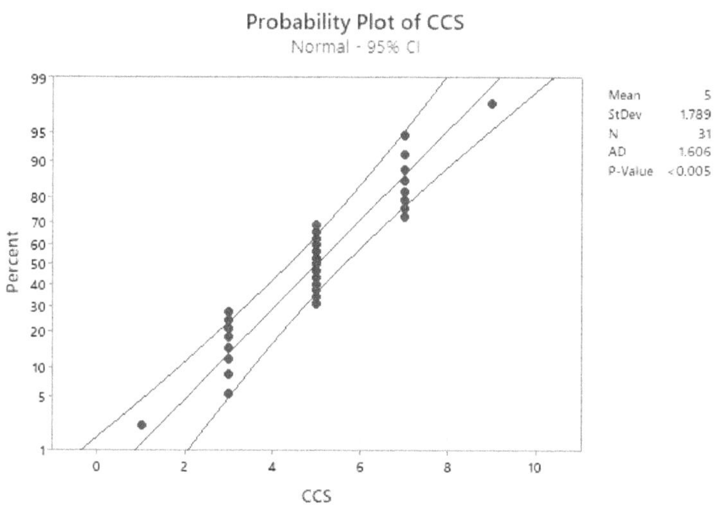

Figure 6.6 Probability plot of CCS.

Surface Plots: Surface plots are very useful to study the effect of two factors on selected CQA so that the optimum compositions of these two factors for desired CQA value can be identified. For example, the effect of MCC in combination with other three factors on dissolution at 15 min is presented in **Figures 6.7 (A, B & C)**.

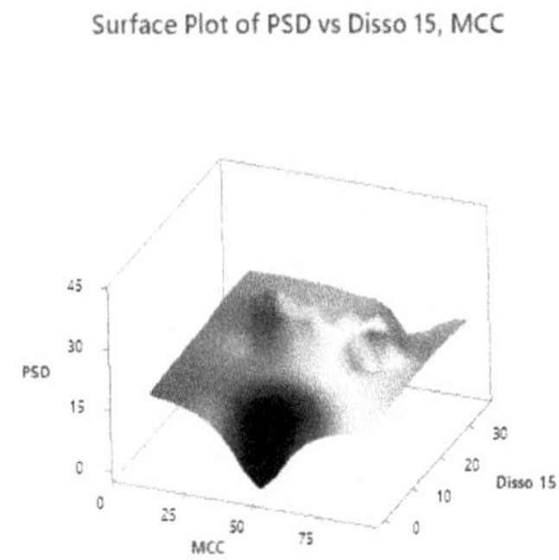

A

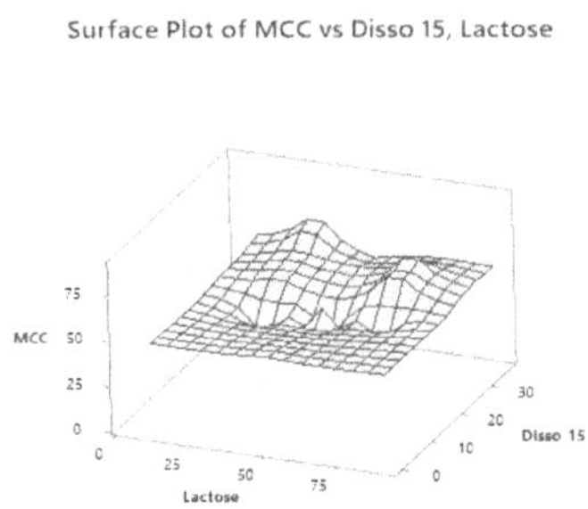

B

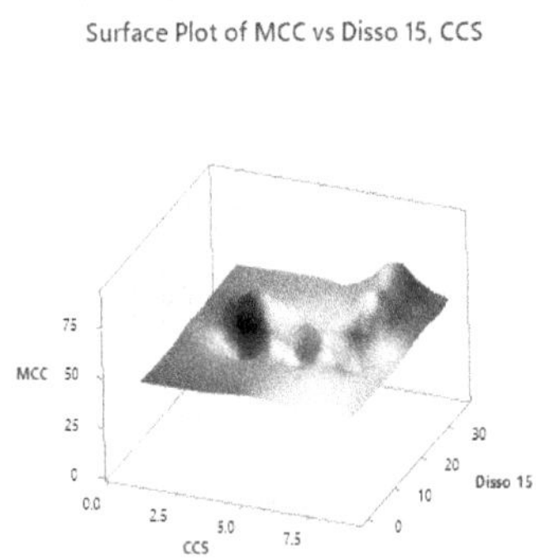

C

Figure 6.7 A- Surface plot of API PSD and MCC for dissolution at 15 min; B- A- Surface plot of MCC and Lactose for dissolution at 15 min; C- A- Surface plot of MCC and CCS for dissolution at 15 min.

The surface response plots are overlaid to identify the design space for each response and all the design spaces for each factor are again overlaid to get final design space for all responses.

Predictability: Once the modelling of the data is completed then the optimization of the response can be arrived by optimizing the excipients composition. The **Figure 6.8 A &B** shows the details of optimization for the current example. The response selected is dissolution at 15 min and desirability is to have maximum response. Similar results can be obtained for other responses. The multiple regression analysis of the data provided the main effect of each factor and also possible combinations of the excipients to obtain highest dissolution at 15 min. Two compositions with PSD 30um and 3 compositions with PSD 20 um of API are presented. It should be noted that the compositions are different from the target composition used to optimize the composition (initial proposed composition). Hence, DoE experiments have provided the solution to the expectation.

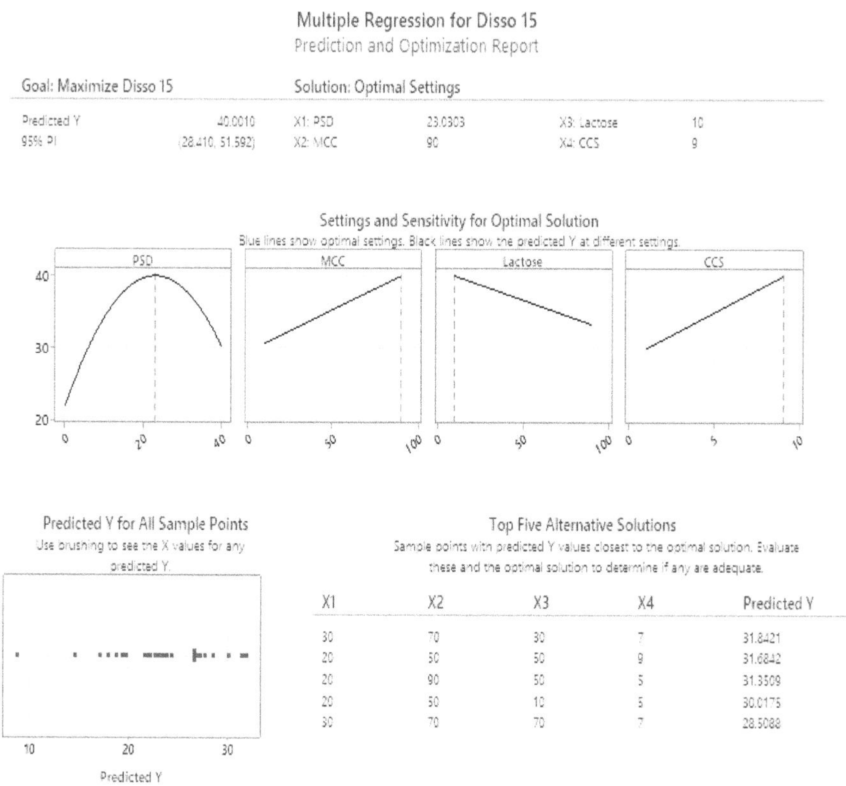

Figure 6.8 A-Multiple regression of data of dissolution at 15 min.

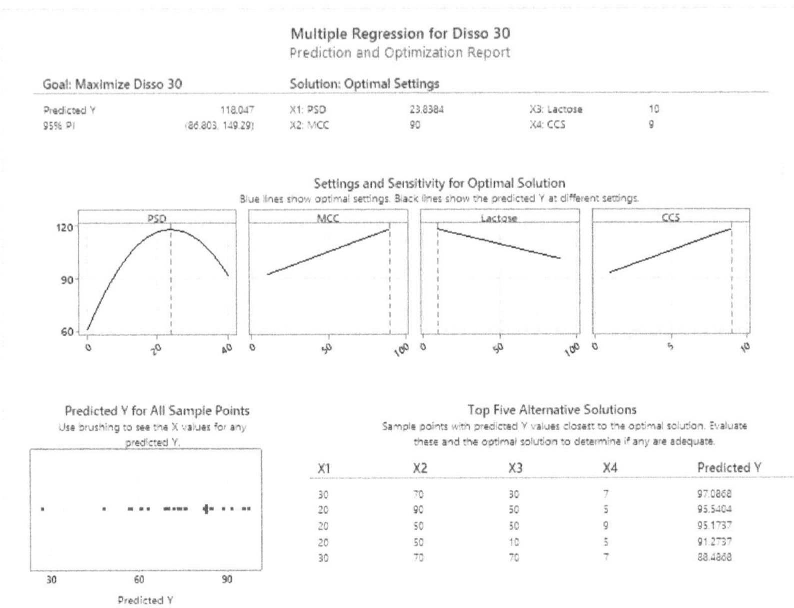

Figure 6.8 B-Multiple regression of data of dissolution at 30 min.

In case of disintegration time, the desirability is to have low DT. **Figure 6.9** shows the multiple regression data of DT and provides the composition that will provide low DT.

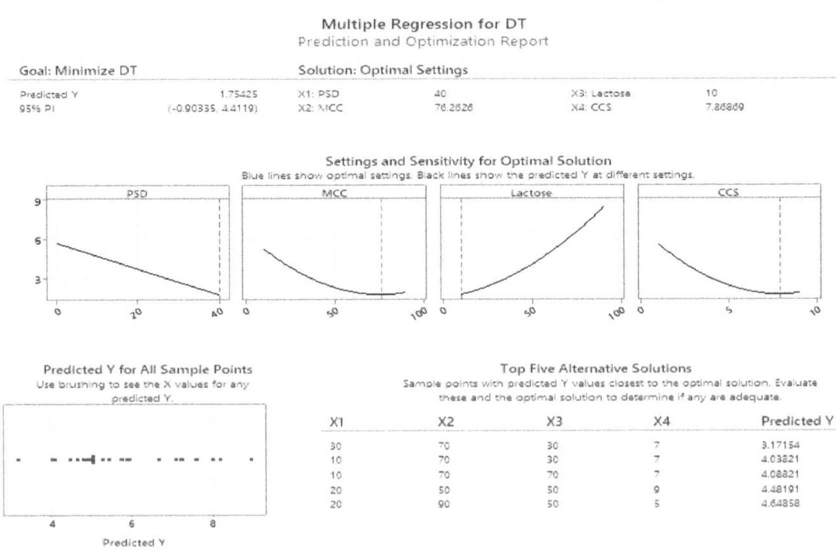

Figure 6.9 Multiple regression of data of disintegration time.

Review of three multiple regression data provides 2 compositions that are common for API PSD of 20um and one composition for 30um. If API PSD is fixed at 20um, two compositions are expected to provide similar DT and dissolution profiles at 15 min and 30min.

Optimized compositions meeting the criteria for DT and dissolution for API PSD of 20um are given in the **Table 6.5**.

Table 6.5 Two optimum compositions for immediate release tablet.

S. No	Component	Functionality	Formula1- Quantity in mg	Formula 2- Quantity in mg
1	API (PSD 20um)	Therapeutic agent	10	10
2	Microcrystalline cellulose (MCC)	Insoluble diluent	50	90
3	Lactose monohydrate	Soluble diluent	50	50
4	Croscarmellose sodium	Disintegrant	9	5
5	Talc	Glidant	2	2
6	Magnesium stearate	Lubricant	1	1
	Total weight of tablet		122	158

Design Space: The counter plots for two factors and one response are considered in fixing the range of each factor that would provide desired response (CQA). For current example, dissolution at 15 min is considered and counter plots for all possible combinations of two factors are generated (**Figure 6.10**). The target drug release is 30% and the factor ranges that would provide 30% release are read from the counter plots in pairs (**Table 6.6**).

Table 6.6 Ranges of factors for 30% dissolution at 15 min.

MCC 10-60	PSD 20-30
MCC 10-90	Lactose 40-60
MCC 10-90	CCS 4-6
PSD 20-30	Lactose 10-65
PSD 20-30	CCS 4-6.2
Lactose 40-60	CCS 1-9

Based on the ranges for each factor listed in table, a common range for each factor that achieves 30% dissolution is decided.

Factor	Acceptable range
PSD	20-30 um
MCC	10-60
Lactose	40-60
CCS	4-6

This process of identifying ranges for each response have to be compiled and the common range for each factor that satisfies all the responses is determined which is nothing but "Design Space".

The regression equations can be used to predict the expected response. For example, the regression equation for dissolution at 15 min is given below.

Disso at 15 min = 11.95 + 0.208 PSD + 0.1167 MCC - 0.0833 Lactose + 1.250 CCS

Let us consider PSD=20, MCC=60, Lactose=40, and CCS= 7 then

Dissolution at 15 min= 11.95+0.208*20+0.1167*60-.0833*40+1.250*7 = 11.95+4.16+7.0-3.33+8.75 = 28.53

Therefore, it is possible to generate complete dissolution profile without manufacturing the tablets but just by using the proposed composition.

So far, the design experiments to optimize composition has been discussed. Process parameters can also be optimized following the same steps used for composition optimization. The process parameters are first identified by Risk analysis and then screening design is used to identify the critical process parameters (CPPs) and these CPPs are further subjected for optimization using response surface methodology (RSM). The experimental data is analysed to create design space for the CPPs. The acceptable CPPs for a desired response can be generated from optimization data. The DoE can also be applied to analytical method development following the step by step process described for composition optimization.

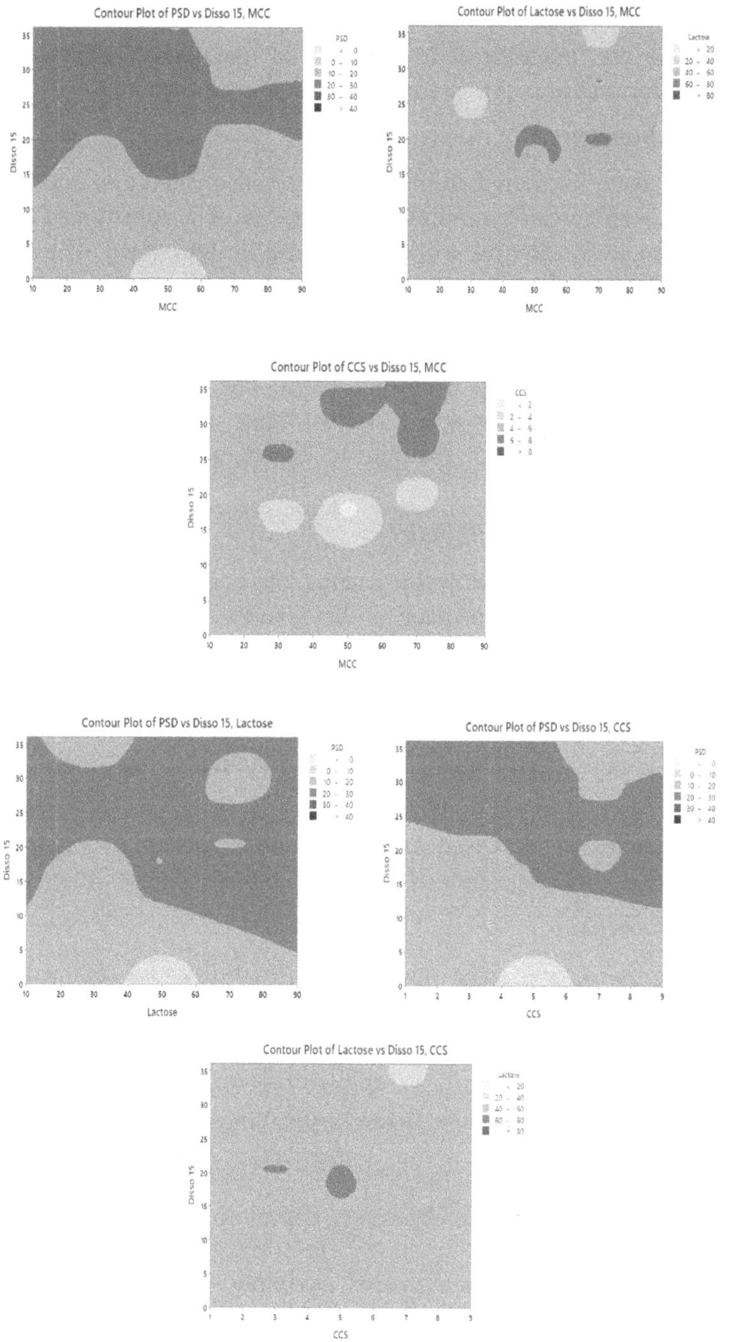

Figure 6.10 Counter plots of factors to identify the working ranges for each factor for dissolution at 15 min.

Advantages of Design Space

There are several advantages in creating design space for pharmaceutical products in formulation, process and analytical methods.

Regulatory Benefits

The design space for composition and process is created and documented in the dossier for submission to regulatory authority. The approval of the dossier allows the manufacturer to work within the design space which is not a deviation. Without design space, the changes are controlled by SUPAC guidance and deviation from composition and process is considered as deviation and some deviations need pre-approval of regulatory authorities before implementation. By operating within the approved Design Space, companies can make minor process adjustments without seeking regulatory approval for each change, leading to faster optimization and reduced administrative burden.

Quality and Performance Benefits

Reproducible Product Quality: In general, the composition and process are fixed in the centre of design space so that small variations would not impact product quality. Hence, consistent product quality is achieved.

Reduced Variability: The CQAs of the product are less variable in design space and hence, minimum variability is observed that leads to fewer rejections and more predictable and reliable manufacturing process.

Optimized Productivity: By identifying optimal process parameters, Design space contributes to increased efficiency and a shorter overall production cycle time.

Economic Benefits

Quick turnaround time: The operational flexibility and reduced need for regulatory submissions for minor changes translate into shorter development and production timelines.

Cost Savings: Reduced waste, lower rejection rates, and optimized processes all contribute to significant cost savings.

Operational Benefits

Thorough Understanding of Product: Creating Design space requires a deep, scientific understanding of the relationship between composition, process parameters and critical quality attributes.

Risk Management: It allows for the systematic exploration of CMAs, CPPs, helping to manage uncertainties and ensure robust manufacturing.

CHAPTER 7

Process Analytical Technology (PAT)

7.1 Introduction to Process Analytical Technology (PAT)

The goal of PAT is to enhance understanding and control the manufacturing process, which is consistent with our current drug quality system: quality cannot be tested into products; it should be built-in or should be by design. The basic principle of QbD is to build quality in drug product by understanding the CMAs and CPPs scientifically that impact the CQAs of drug product and not to test end product. The term *analytical* in PAT is viewed broadly to include chemical, physical, microbiological, mathematical, and risk analysis conducted in an integrated manner. Hence, Process Analytical Technology (PAT) is used to design, analyse, and control manufacturing processes in real-time by measuring critical quality and performance attributes of raw materials and in-process materials to ensure final product quality. US FDA has issued a guidance on PAT.

Measurement of specific characteristics of raw material, blend, or process parameter in-line or on-line using proper instruments enables continuous quality control, provides deep process understanding, optimizes processes for efficiency and cost-effectiveness. Chemometrics are used in PAT. Chemometrics is a field that uses mathematical and statistical methods to extract meaningful information from chemical data. It's an interdisciplinary science combining chemistry, statistics, mathematics, and computer science to improve chemical analysis, design experiments, calibrate instruments, and interpret complex data from chemical systems.

Instruments used in Process Analytical Technology (PAT) include spectroscopic tools like Near-Infrared (NIR) and Raman spectroscopy, particle size analysers such as focussed bean reflectance measurement (FBRM), chromatography, mass spectrometers, and fundamental sensors for temperature, pressure, and pH. These in-situ or online tools provide real-time data for understanding, monitoring, and controlling chemical and physical aspects of processes without a need to collect samples and analyse offline.

This data is inspected, transformed, and modelled using multivariate, artificial intelligence (AI) and machine learning methods to detect trends, predict outcomes, and enable immediate process adjustments or real-time release testing. Key goals include enhancing process understanding, improving operational efficiency, reducing reliance on offline testing, and ensuring product quality throughout the manufacturing lifecycle.

7.2 Tools and Techniques

Various advanced instruments are used in PAT and the collected data is analysed by various mathematical and statistical tools. **Table 7.1** provides most important instruments and their application.

Table 7.1 Various instruments used in PAT.

Instrument	Applications
Spectroscopic Methods	
Near-Infrared Spectroscopy (NIRS)	Blend uniformity, content uniformity and moisture content
Raman Spectroscopy	Raw materials identification, and quantitative analysis.
Fourier Transform Infrared (FTIR) Spectroscopy	Raw materials identification, and quantitative analysis.
Terahertz (THz) Imaging	Monitors film coating thickness and pore size in tablets.
Spatial Filter Velocimetry (SFV)	Estimates particle chord length using the particle's shadow.
Focused Beam Reflectance Measurement (FBRM)	Measures particles length in solution to monitor nucleation during crystallization of compounds.
Acoustic Resonance Spectrometry (ARS)	Analyses sound generated during the process to determine tablet properties like mass and thickness.
Imaging Techniques	
Hyperspectral Imaging (HIS)	Provides spectral and chemical imaging for a deeper understanding of the process.
Optical Coherence Tomography (OCT)	The tablet internal structures are captured as images.

Table 7.1 ***Contd...***

Instrument	Applications
Other techniques	
Mass Spectrometry (MS)	Quantitative analysis of API and other critical components
Microwave Resonance Technology (MRT)	Monitors water content and correlates with granule size in fluid bed drying and wet granulation.
Drag Force Flow Sensors (DFFS)	Measures wet mass consistency during wet granulation process.

Near-Infrared Spectroscopy (NIRS)

Near-Infrared (NIR) spectroscopy is a widely used, fast, and non-destructive analytical technique that serves as a key Process Analytical Technology (PAT) tool for real-time, in-line monitoring and control of manufacturing processes. NIRS enables the rapid determination of quality attributes such as drug concentration, blend homogeneity, and moisture content without the need for extensive sampling or destructive testing.

For example, a blending operation is carried out wherein API and other excipients are mixed to obtain a uniform blend of all components. An NIR probe is placed in the blend and the blender operation is initiated. NIR light is passed through or reflected of the sample and the spectra are recorded continuously with time of operation of blender. Molecules absorb specific wavelengths of NIR light based on their vibrational frequencies, generating a unique spectral "fingerprint". Chemometrics are used to interpret the complex NIR spectra, extracting meaningful information about various chemical and physical properties. This real-time data generated provides instant feedback on CQAs allowing immediate adjustments to the process.

Raman Spectroscopy

This technique is similar to NIRS but the principle on which works is different. The Raman probes are placed in the sample during operation to collect real-time data. A laser light illuminates a sample, and the light scattered off the molecules is analysed to create a unique spectrum, or "fingerprint," for each substance. It is highly sensitive and provides each component data quantitatively but very costly instrument. The data analysis and use are similar to NIRS.

Fourier Transform Infrared (FTIR) Spectroscopy

By measuring infrared light absorption, FTIR generates a unique molecular "fingerprint" for each substance, enabling the identification and quantification of chemicals without extensive sample preparation. The resulting spectrum provides a unique molecular fingerprint based on absorption peaks related to the sample's chemical functional groups. This "fingerprint" allows for the identification of substances and the quantification of their concentration in a mixture.

The real-time data generated is processed similar to that of NIRS.

Terahertz (THz) Imaging

Terahertz imaging advantages include non-ionizing radiation, unique spectral fingerprints for material identification, and the ability to provide 3D internal structural information, which is invaluable for quality control, such as determining tablet coating integrity. THz waves interact with matter at a molecular level, revealing unique "spectral fingerprints" for different chemicals and materials. THz imaging can penetrate materials, creating 3D internal images and revealing structural details like cracks, embedded layers, or variations in blend uniformity that are not visible with optical methods. THz imaging provides detailed information on the uniformity, thickness, and integrity of tablet coatings. It can detect internal features such as cracks or localized chemical agglomerations within a tablet.

Spatial Filter Velocimetry

Spatial Filter Velocimetry (SFV) is a Process Analytical Technology (PAT) tool that monitors particle size, shape, and velocity in real-time during manufacturing processes like granulation and coating. A parallel laser beam is passed through the sample containing particles, creating a shadow that a linear fibre-optic array detects as a pulse signal. The pulse's time of flight and particle's velocity are measured simultaneously and chord length is calculated by SFV. This measurement is in-line and non-invasive in nature used in quality control of solid dosage form manufacturing.

Focused Beam Reflectance Measurement (FBRM)

A laser probe is placed in the sample during the operation to perform in-situ, real-time particle size and count analysis by measuring the "chord length" of particles as they intersect a rotating laser beam. The chord length distribution called CLD is generated from the collected information. CLD is sensitive to the changes in particle size, count, and shape. This allows real-time monitoring and control of processes like granulation, flocculation and crystallization. The online data analysis helps to predict and ensure desired particle characteristics, leading to improved process development and consistency.

Acoustic Resonance Spectrometry (ARS)

A transmitter generates vibrations and these vibrations interact with the sample, causing it to resonate at its natural frequencies. A receiver detects the resulting acoustic signal generated due to the vibration induced by the transmitter. The time-based signal is transformed into a frequency spectrum using Fast Fourier Transform (FFT). Principle component analysis (PCA) or other pattern recognition techniques are applied to the spectral data to identify features and classify samples.

Hyperspectral Imaging (HSI)

Each material has a unique spectral fingerprint that identifies its composition. HSI analyses these signatures to distinguish and identify substances. The HSI covers both visible and infrared spectrum of waves. A hyperspectral camera collects spectrum and divides the spectrum into many narrow bands, creating a three-dimensional "hyper cube" where each pixel has its own unique spectral signature. HIS captures both spatial and spectral information from an object, providing a detailed view of its chemical and physical properties.

HSI enables non-destructive, real-time monitoring of pharmaceutical products and processes, supporting continuous manufacturing and quality assurance. Modern machine learning techniques allow for rapid analysis of hyperspectral data, enabling online or real-time operation.

Optical Coherence Tomography (OCT)

OCT provides non-invasive, high-resolution, real-time, cross-sectional imaging of the internal microstructure of materials in various industrial settings, particularly in pharmaceutical tablet coating.

The near-infrared light is used to create cross-sectional images of a sample by measuring the interference of backscattered light from internal structures. The near infrared light not only provides images of surface but also the internal structure by penetrating below the surface to different lengths. This allows for the detection of internal structures, layer thickness of coat, and homogeneity within semi-transparent materials. Advanced instruments offer high speed and high-resolution images for real-time process monitoring and enabling immediate quality control, defect identification, and process optimization.

Mass Spectrometry (MS)

The specialized Mass Spectrometer is coupled with PAT for online/real-time analysis of samples. This technology is useful for monitoring complex mixtures, including gases, and provides valuable information for controlling processes like distillation, drying etc.

Samples, such as gases in a headspace during distillation or drying or liquid sample from a reaction mixture, are introduced into the mass spectrometer, often after minimal preparation. Molecules in the sample are ionized, and these ions are then separated based on their mass-to-charge (m/z) ratio. The resulting mass spectrum provides a unique "fingerprint" of the compounds present. The complex data obtained is analysed by computer-based software to identify and quantify specific components in the sample. The presence and quantity of starting materials, intermediates, product, impurities, and other by-products are monitored on real-time basis.

Microwave Resonance Technology (MRT)

The wavelength range for microwaves is from 1 millimetre (mm) to 1 meter (m) which corresponds to 300 megahertz (MHz) to 300 gigahertz (GHz). This range is in between radio and infrared wavelength ranges. This range of electromagnetic radiation is used in MRT and the interaction of these waves with water is the basis for quantitative estimation of water content in a sample. The derived MRT signal is a band whose frequency peak and bandwidth decrease as water and material load increase. By analysing multiple resonance frequencies, MRT can provide moisture values that are independent of product density. Temperature has an influence on the signal and hence, a thermocouple is placed to measure the temperature of sample and appropriate correction is made to provide exact values of water content. MRT is used for in-line monitoring of moisture and, to some extent, density in industrial processes, particularly for granules in pharmaceutical fluidized-bed granulation.

Drag Force Flow Sensors (DFFS)

A probe, hollow cylindrical pin, is immersed in the sample during operation and as the fluid or powder flows around the probe, it exerts a drag force on probe which causes deflection of probe. Optical gauges or similar technologies are used to precisely measure the minute deflection of the probe. The extent of deflection is directly related to the flow force, which is a function of the material's velocity, particle density, and viscosity.

DFF sensors provide real-time, continuous monitoring of processes like high-shear wet granulation, enabling precise control over granule properties and offering a sensitive tool for formulation development and manufacturing within the pharmaceutical and other industries.

7.3 Real Time Monitoring and Controls

The purpose of PAT is to monitor the CMAs and CPPs on real time basis and provide feedback to adjust the process parameters so that the quality of product is maintained proactively. The steps involved in achieving this objective are continuous measurement of CMA or CPP or both, quick analysis of acquired data, feedback to control the CMA or CPP or both within acceptable value, control of parameters within specified range and online documentation of these events.

Continuous Measurement

Sensors are used directly within the process stream (in-line), at the periphery of the stream (at-line), or periodically near the stream (online) to collect continuous data. The important process variables such as temperature, pH, viscosity, and composition are constantly monitored.

Quick analysis of acquired data

Quick data analysis in Process Analytical Technology (PAT) uses real-time, in-line measurements and advanced analytical tools like spectroscopy and chemometrics to continuously monitor critical quality attributes (CQAs) during manufacturing. This real-time data is then fed into statistical process control (SPC) models or machine learning algorithms to provide rapid feedback and enable swift process adjustments, ensuring product quality, improving efficiency, and facilitating real-time product release.

Feedback loop

By constantly monitoring the process and feeding information back to control systems, feedback loops facilitate continuous control and real-time quality assurance, leading to improved process understanding, reduced variability, and more efficient, automated manufacturing.

Control of Parameters

PAT tools, like spectroscopy and chromatography, provide in-line, at-line, or online data that feeds into control systems, such as statistical process control (SPC), to adjust parameters like temperature, speed, and pressure within defined limits. This real-time monitoring and control leads to enhanced product quality, reduced waste, and more efficient manufacturing.

Online documentation

Online documentation for Process Analytical Technology (PAT) within a Quality by Design (QbD) framework includes the FDA Guidance for Industry on PAT, scientific publications, and manufacturer documentation for PAT instruments. Key documentation elements are design space definitions, Critical Quality Attributes (CQAs), risk assessments, process monitoring data, multivariate data analysis (MVDA) models, and documentation for the entire PAT model lifecycle.

7.4 Enhanced Process Understanding

Process Analytical Technology (PAT) enhances understanding of a process within the Quality by Design (QbD) framework by providing real-time, in-situ data on critical quality and performance attributes, enabling better process design, control, and continuous improvement. In pharmaceutical manufacturing several unit operations are used as a continuous chain. Each process output is an input to the next unit operation, hence, each unit process is controlled using PAT so as to produce consistent quality output. This data-driven approach moves beyond traditional offline testing to allow for timely decisions, leading to more robust processes, consistent product quality, and the establishment of a well-defined design space.

PAT enables comprehensive knowledge of how material attributes and process parameters influence product quality, identifying relationships between variables and outcomes. PAT data helps in identifying and defining Design Space, which is the range of process parameters where the process consistently produces quality products. Adoptive process controls and predictive modelling ensures that process parameters stay within the design space and meets quality thus creating a robust process.

By deeply understanding the process and applying science-based tools, PAT enables manufacturers to achieve greater process efficiency, product consistency, and reduced costs through improved process control and continuous improvement, shifting from testing after manufacturing to building quality in from the start.

7.5 Regulatory Framework

"US FDA considers PAT to be a system for designing, analysing, and controlling manufacturing through timely measurements (i.e., during processing) of critical quality and performance attributes of raw and in-process materials and processes, with the goal of ensuring final product quality."

Pharmaceutical manufacturing will need to employ innovation, cutting edge scientific and engineering knowledge, along with the best principles of quality management to respond to the challenges of new discoveries and ways of doing business (e.g., individualized therapy, genetically tailored treatment).

The FDA released the guidance "PAT — A Framework for Innovative Pharmaceutical Development, Manufacturing, and Quality Assurance," which outlines the principles and expectations for implementing PAT within a QbD framework. This framework provides a science-based approach, encouraging the industry to use PAT for understanding, controlling, and assuring the quality of drug products throughout their lifecycle. Key regulatory expectations include systematic risk assessment, the establishment of a Quality Target Product Profile (QTPP), identifying Critical Quality Attributes (CQAs) and Critical Process Parameters (CPPs), and the continuous monitoring of processes to ensure adherence to a defined design space and potentially enable real-time release testing.

The framework is rooted in QbD, which emphasizes that quality should be designed into the product and process, not just tested at the end. The goal is to develop a deep understanding of the manufacturing process so it can be continuously monitored and controlled. A crucial step in the QbD-aligned PAT development process is performing a thorough quality risk assessment to identify potential hazards and implement appropriate controls. The framework supports CPV, where the process is continuously monitored and evaluated to ensure consistent product quality and allow for rapid intervention when negative trends are detected. A significant benefit is the ability to perform real-time release testing, which provides earlier assurance of product quality and reduces the need to hold or destroy batches.

The PAT frame work is to design composition and processes for the manufacture of drug product by understanding the processes and come up with design space within which the quality of product is maintained. Continuous monitoring of CQAs during the process and providing feedback loop to adjust the process parameters within the proved operational range so to reduce risks to quality and regulatory concerns while improving efficiency.

Advantages of PAT

Implementation of PAT gives high quality product, safety and efficiency of the manufacturing process. The process understanding and product quality control increases with PAT. The advantages of implementation of PAT in pharmaceutical industry are listed below.

1. Creation of Design Space: The optimization of the process parameters provides clear operational range for each process parameter and provides design space within which the process parameters always produce quality drug product.
2. Increased automation to improve operator safety and reduce human errors due PAT implementation.
3. Reduction in production cycle times by using on-, in-, and/or at-line measurements and controls.
4. Reducing rejects, scrap, and re-processing of the failed products which is a common occurrence in old type of process.
5. Since PAT is mainly uses on-line or in-line testing, a real time release of drug product to the market possible avoiding delayed release of product to the market due to testing of finished product.
6. Improves conservation of energy, materials, increases capacity and efficiency of the process.
7. The management of process becomes simple with less variation leading to quality product with desired specifications.
8. PAT facilitates continuous process improvement with the data collected for several batches manufactured.

Case Study: Use of PAT tool Drag Force Flow Sensor (DFFS) in High Shear Wet Granulation.

Most of the tablets are manufactured by wet granulation process using RMG that induces high shear during wet granulation. The purpose of study is to understand the force generated in the granulation process that can be used as a surrogate to fix the binder concentration and to define end point of granulation.

The formula proposed for granulation is given below.

Ingredient	Grade	Percent used	Functionality
Microcrystalline cellulose	Avicel PH 101	61	Insoluble diluent
Lactose	Anhydrous	37	Soluble diluent
Croscarmellose sodium	AcDiSol	1	Disintegrant
Hydroxypropyl Cellulose (HPC)	Klucel EXF	1	Binder

Granulation fluid: The objective of the study is to optimize the percent of HPC in the composition and hence, 1%, 3% and 5% levels are selected for the study. The excess amount of HPC was compensated with the decrease in MCC amount accordingly. Pure water was used as the granulating fluid. The fluid uptake was fixed at 40% of total weight of excipients for wet granulation.

Rapid Mixer Granulator (RMG): The RMG selected is having three impeller blades and a chopper. The impeller speed and chopper speed are fixed throughout the process. The lid has provisions to insert DFFS probe, Thermocouple, and pure water spray. **Figure 7.1a** is the RMG with DFFS fixed in it.

Drag Force Flow Sensor (DFFS): The sensor is a thin, hollow, cylindrical needle, approximately 3mm diameter. The base of the sensor deflects when flow force from the material in which it is placed exerts on it. The optical strain gauges measure the force experienced by the base of the sensor and generates signal. The thermocouple placed in the RMG measures the temperature simultaneously and feeds into the algorithm to make relevant corrections in the signal generated by optical strain gauge since the force is affected by temperature of the mass (**Figure 7.1b**)

The small diameter of the sensor offers minimal intrusion to the flow of material and high frequency measurement rates of up to 500 samples per second. This allows on-line measurement directly from the mass during the entire process. The probe is placed 2.5cm into the mass and about 8 cm from the periphery of RMG (almost in the middle of the impeller blade).

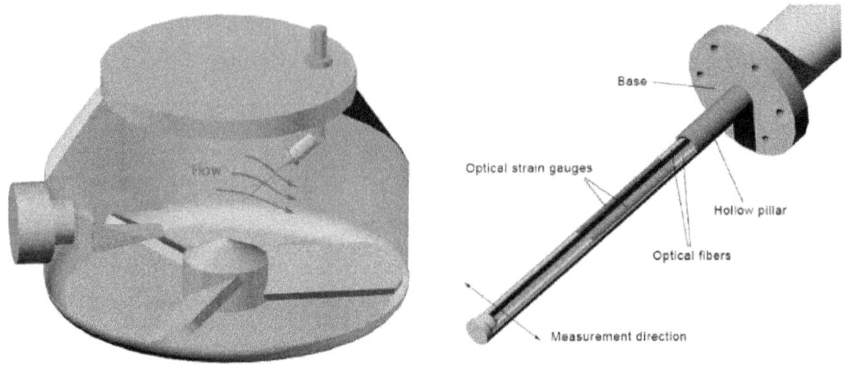

Figure 7.1 (a) Rapid mixer granulator & (b) DFFS probe.

Experimental Design: The composition of MCC, Lactose and CCS are fixed and also the fluid uptake is fixed at 40% of the materials weight. The dry mixing time is 4 minutes and binder solution addition time is 3 minutes. The kneading time after the addition of pure water is for 5 minutes with variable HPC concentration of 1%, 3% and 5%. Triplicate experiments were conducted to check the consistency of the results.

Data Collection: The data is collected from the start of dry mixing for 4 minutes, binder addition for 3 minutes and kneading for 5 minutes. Time used for dry mixing is designated with negative sign.

The force exerted on probe during granulation process has maximum value when one of the blades is below the probe and minimum value when the probe is between the two blades. The difference between these forces is called "force pulse magnitude (FPM)". FPM is a differential measurement and hence provides a reliable characteristic of the wet mass consistency and densification because it is independent from possible zero drift in the raw signal.

Data Analysis: A plot of time versus FPM is used to understand the characteristics of the mass in RMG during the operation. The shadowed area is the binder addition time **Figure 7.2**. It can be observed that the maximum FPM value is just after the completion of the addition of binder solution

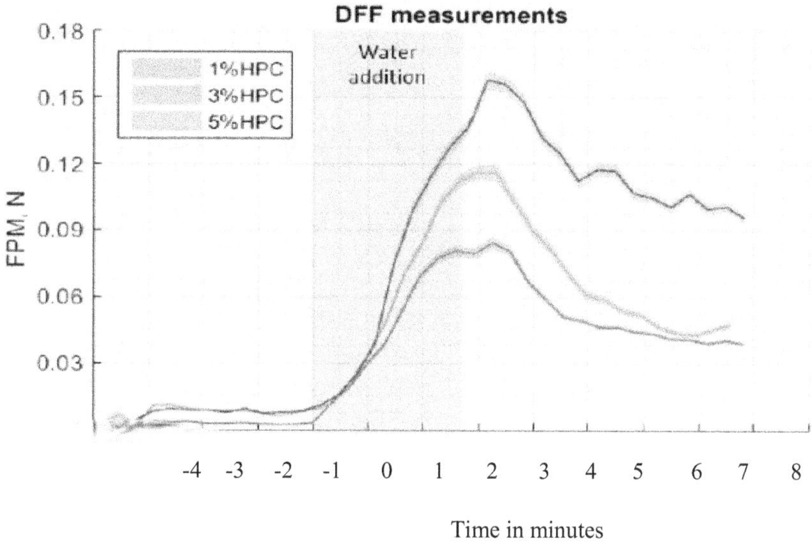

Figure 7.2 Time versus FPM plot.

Optimization of the process: The wet granulation mass is now dried using fluid bed drier and the dried granules are evaluated for their characteristics such as PSD, granule density, and flowability. The results indicate that 3% HPC is useful in achieving the desired CQAs. Now the granulation end point is optimized by collecting the wet granular mass at 1, 3 and 5 minutes and evaluating the resultant dried granules. The kneading time was found to be 3 minutes and now the range of FPM value (0.035 to 0.045) is fixed as end point of granulation. Subsequent batches shall be manufacture with the end point of granulation falling in the specified range of FPM value and ignores the kneading time since variation in raw materials CMAs may influence the time of kneading but not the end point detected by PAT.

CHAPTER 8

Scale Up of Manufacturing Process

The research and development of a drug product manufacturing involves establishment of pharmaceutical composition, an array of unit operations combined in an order, and finished product specifications. The laboratory scale equipment is relatively small compared with those used in commercial manufacturing but efforts are made to use same type of equipment with respect to geometry and mechanism of operation. Most of the manufacturing processes used for drug products are batch processes. FDA define the batch as "A specific quantity of a drug or other material produced according to a single manufacturing order during the same cycle of manufacture and intended to have uniform character and quality, within specified limits". Process is defined as "A series of operations and/or actions used to produce a desired result". Scale up is mainly referred to the size of operation compared to the one used in research laboratory.

During the drug product development, the composition of a dosage form is finalized and the manufacturing process is optimized using the laboratory equipment. In general, the pharmaceutical composition is fixed and is *scale independent*. But the commercial production of drug product utilizes bigger equipment than those used in laboratory. Therefore, there is a need for systematic and scientific investigation to scale up the manufacturing process from laboratory scale to commercial scale. This chapter is focussed on the scale up of pharmaceutical product manufacturing process.

The manufacturing process for pharmaceutical product involves a series of unit operations that are performed sequentially to finally produce finished product. For example, manufacture of immediate release tablets contains blending, wet granulation in rapid mixer granulator, drying of wet mass by fluid bed processor, milling, sieving, blending, lubrication, and compression. The finished product quality depends on all these unit operations. The first unit operation, blending in this case, uses raw materials whose critical material attributes (CMAs) are important and the output of this unit operation is to give uniform distribution of all the components of the mixture. This uniformity is mainly checked by analysing the drug content in the samples collected. The blend assay and blend uniformity are critical quality attributes

(CQAs) of output material from blender, and they are the CMAs to the next operation, RMG granulation. Therefore, specifications are defined for blend assay and blend uniformity to ensure that blending operation gives the blend that meets the specifications. Since, the performance of a unit operation depends on the scale of operation, there is a need to optimize the unit operation at a bigger scale.

The critical process parameters (CPPs) of a unit operation influence the output from the operation and these CPPs are divided into scale independent and scale dependent. Scale independent process parameters are those process parameters that remain constant across the size of the batch. However, scale dependent parameters have to be optimized based on the batch size. All the CPPs are optimized at laboratory scale and hence, only scale dependent process parameters have to be optimized for the larger batch size. Therefore, list of scale dependent and independent parameters for each unit operation have to be prepared. Let us consider blending operation and **Table 8.1** shows the list of scale independent and dependent critical process parameters. It is assumed that the geometry of blender is similar to that used in laboratory, order of addition of components into blender and the environment in the manufacturing area are not CPPs.

Table 8.1 Scale dependent and independent CPPs for Blending.

Critical Process Parameter	**Scale Dependent/Independent**
Blender RPM	Dependent
Blending Time	Dependent
Tip Speed	Independent
Number of revolutions	Independent
Occupancy	Independent

Scale up based on Engineering Principles - Blending

Before attempting any trials, it is necessary to use engineering principles to calculate CPPs values. The important principles are maintaining similarity between the laboratory scale CPPs and larger scale CPPs.

Geometric Similarity

This involves maintaining consistent ratios between different dimensions of the blender, such as the height-to-diameter ratio (H/D) where H is the height of the material in the blender and D is the diameter of the blender.

Dynamic Similarity

This principle focuses on maintaining similar force distributions and flow patterns by keeping dimensionless numbers constant, like Froude number (ratio of centrifugal force to gravitation force). This is useful when impeller is used to mix the materials and liquids.

Kinematic Similarity

This principle involves maintaining similar velocity fields, which can be achieved by keeping tip speed constant.

Calculation of Froude number:

The blender in the lab has a radius of 0.1m and operated at 60 RPM or 1 rotation per second (RPS). The equation for Froude number for blender is given below.

$$Fr = r^*n^2/g \qquad .....(8.1)$$

Where Fr = Froude number; r is the radius of blender on rotational axis in meters, n are rotations per second (RPS) and g is gravitational force in m/s^2 (9.81).

$$Fr = (0.1*1*1)/9.81 = 0.012$$

Now the rotational speed of big blender selected for commercial manufacturing is determined using its dimensions and equating Froude number. The big blender has 0.45m radius.

Fr = 0.012, r=0.45 and hence, n has to be calculated using Eq.8.1.

$$n^2 = (Fr^*g)/r \qquad .....(8.2) \text{ and}$$

$$n = \sqrt{}(Fr^*g)/r \qquad .....(8.3)$$

Hence, n=√(0.012*9.81)/0.45 = √0.2616 = 0.5115 RPS and by multiplying it with 60 to convert it into RPM, =0.5115*60= 30.69.

The blender rotational speed is selected as 30 RPM.

The another important CPP is the blending time at 30 RPM in commercial scale blender. Hence, an experiment is designed to run the blender at 30 RPM and samples are collected at defined time intervals and analysed for CQAs such as blend uniformity, blend assay and flow characters. The time range within which the CQAs meet the defined specifications is identified for regular manufacturing process.

Similarly, all other unit operations in the manufacturing process are optimized at commercial scale so that drug product can be manufactured regularly that provides defined quality. PAT tools are highly useful in the optimization of CPPs of a unit operation.

Scale up based on PAT tools - Blending

NIR Spectroscopy for on-line measurement of blending operation: As explained in previous chapter on PAT tools, NIR spectroscopy is simple, versatile, cost effective and on-line measurement tool for optimization of unit operation. NIR spectrometer equipped with NIR tunable laser sources and detector were used for this study. For on-line measurements, the spectrometer was securely mounted onto a lid and location was similar to the one described above for DFFS. NIR spectra were recorded for each revolution of blender. 4 spectra co-averaged into 1 spectrum to be acquired in each revolution. Measured NIR spectral data were then transmitted via a wireless network from the spectrometer unit to a nearby laptop. The recording was continued for 200 revolutions to find out the blend uniformity for each revolution. The percent of drug in the blend was estimated based on NIR data for each revolution. **Figure 8.1** shows the percent of drug in the blend against the number of revolutions.

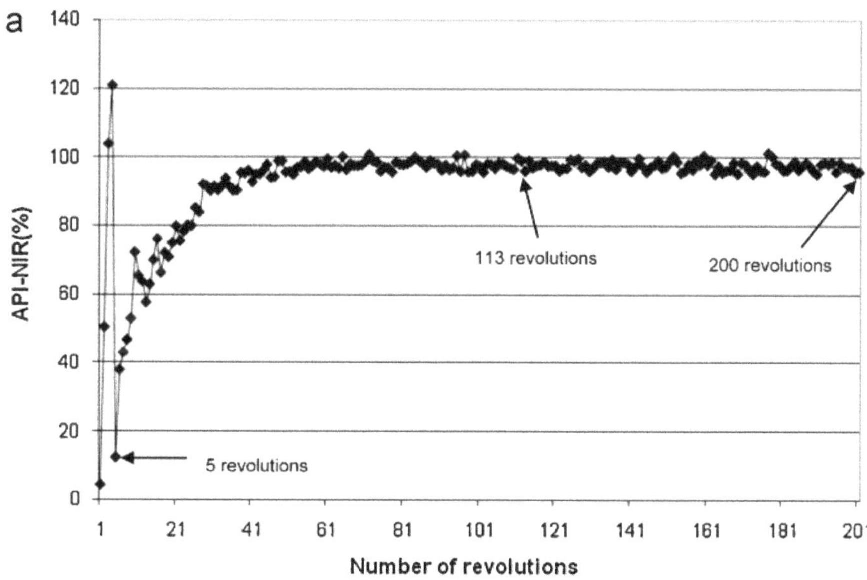

Figure 8.1 Percent of API in the blend versus number of revolutions.

It can be seen from the plot that from 61 revolutions onwards the API percent is almost 100. Hence, the blending time can be fixed safely from 80 to 120 revolutions that translates into 2.67 minutes to 4 minutes (blending time = Number of revolutions/RPM). However, the process is monitored online during the manufacturing so that once 100% API is found in blend, the operation can be stopped.

Scale up based on Engineering Principles – Wet Granulation using RMG

Rapid mixer granulator is routinely used in the wet granulation process to achieve uniformity of all components and proper bonding to form granules that have good properties of granule strength, porosity, density and flow properties. The process is optimized at the laboratory scale by studying all the CPPs of the process. The scale up of the process at the commercial scale needs further optimization for the scale dependent process parameters. The **Table 8.2** shows the scale dependent and independent process parameters of the wet granulation process using RMG.

Table 8.2 Scale Dependent and Independent CPPs of Wet Granulation by RMG.

Critical Process Parameter	Scale Dependent/Independent
Impeller speed	Dependent
Fluid uptake	Independent
Binder addition time	Dependent
Kneading time	Dependent
Chopper speed	Independent
Occupancy	Independent

The engineering principles that are applied to the critical process parameters during the scale up are related to geometric, dynamic and kinematic similarities as explained above.

Geometric similarity: The geometric similarity is related to the granulator bowl configuration, which includes bowl occupation and geometry, as well as the impeller configuration and chopper design. The same ratio of linear dimensions is required to ensure geometric similarity between the lab scale and commercial scale RMGs.

The ratio of linear dimensions is required to ensure geometric similarity. The height of the dry blend in the RMG (H) to the diameter of the impeller(D) are used to calculate H/D ratio. This value should be kept constant across the scale. Hence, the H/D value used in laboratory scale should be applied to commercial scale. The diameter of the impeller of commercial equipment is used and the height of the dry blend is fixed so as to maintain constant H/D ratio across the scale. So $Hl/Dl = Hc/Dc$ where l denotes lab scale and c denotes commercial scale.

Kinematic similarity: Kinematic similarities are related to the velocities and timescale ratios, for example, the impeller tip speed should be constant. The tip speed of the impeller used in lab scale should maintained in commercial scale also. It means the tip speeds of both the scale should be same.

$$\text{Tip speed of impeller} = \prod * Dl * Nl \quad .....(8.4)$$

Where, Dl is the diameter of the impeller in lab scale, and Nl is RPM used in lab scale. If the diameter of impeller in commercial scale is Dc then the RPM for commercial scale can be calculated.

$$Dl*Nl = Dc*Nc \quad .....(8.5)$$

Hence, $$Nc = Dl*Nl/Dc \quad .....(8.6)$$

If the Dl = 0.5m and Nl = 100 and Dc = 1.25m then the Nc = 0.5*100/1.25 = 40 RPM

Hence, 40 RPM is used in commercial scale for wet granulation. Some scientists suggest to maintain constant Froude number across the scales.

Dynamic similarity: Dynamic similarities refer to the forces experienced by the particles during granulation, maintaining internal particle flow constant. The shear experienced by the particles is derived mainly from particle-particle, particle-wall, particle-impeller, and particle-chopper collisions. This approach ensures consistent energy input to the material being mixed by keeping the power per unit volume (P/V) constant, which is a more advanced method when geometric and kinetic similarity are not feasible. This involves complex calculations using the power Number (Np) and material density (ρ), often requiring more detailed engineering data.

The practical approach in the scale up of a process is to use RMG having similar geometry, impeller and chopper design, occupancy (fill volume) and use tip speed of impeller equal to that used in laboratory scale. Binder addition method is generally by spraying and the spray rate decides the binder addition time. The other scale dependent process parameters (Binder addition time, fluid up take and kneading time) have to be discussed.

Binder solution addition method: The binder solution addition at lab scale is practised by pouring but binder solution addition using spray system is recommended. The nucleation for the granule growth depends on the wetting of powder by binder solution. In order to achieve uniform and more reproducible granulation is to use mechanically controlled spray system. The critical parameters are the volume of binder solution, the diameter of the droplets generated, and the spray area. One of the approaches is to maintain dimensionless spray flux (ψ_a) as defined by the **equation 8.7**.

$$\psi_a = 3V/(2A*d_d) \quad .....(8.7)$$

Where, V= volumetric flow rate of binder solution, A= area of spray zone and d_d= diameter of the droplets generated. It has been suggested to keep ψ_a lower than 0.1.

Granulating Fluid Amount: The granulating fluid amount required for proper granulation depends on the properties of the dry blend and hence, it is considered to be dependent on the formulation which should not change during scale up. The fluid amount is strongly dependent on the formulation, and wet granulation behaviour is highly dependent on the powder's physical properties. Varying binder solution amounts are evaluated at laboratory scale to understand the optimum amount to achieve desired properties of granules and an optimum amount of binder solution is selected. The scale-up is usually proportional, keeping constant the powder-to-liquid ratio, and assuming an optimal granulating fluid amount as determined in the lab scale. However, it is generally observed that slight deviation in amount of fluid from the lab scale to higher scale occurs. The binder solution amount is usually adjusted to compensate for other scale up related inaccuracies and maintain particle velocity and force distribution across the scales.

Kneading time: The time required for granulation after the completion of binder solution addition is called kneading time or wet massing time. In general, it is maintained constant across the scales since tip speed of the impeller is matched at all the scales. If the impeller speed is scaled up by a constant tip speed, the total number of rotations criterion would result in a wet massing time proportional to the bowl diameters. It has been recommended to keep kneading time as short as possible.

A scale up trial is conducted by keeping geometric, kinematic and dynamic similarity to the possible extent. It means, the granulators have similar geometry, impeller and chopper design, occupancy, impeller tip speed, binder addition rate, binder amount and kneading time. The samples are collected at the end of kneading time and subjected for evaluation and some portion of wet mass is dried using any drier with fixed parameter and evaluated for the critical quality attributes of dried granules and compared with laboratory scale data. Based on the results, a second scale up study may be required with revised process parameters.

Scale up based on PAT tools – Rapid Mixer Granulator (RMG)

In order to determine the end point of granulation, dynamic image analysis is useful in determining the granule size distribution during kneading time in RMG. The QicPic is a dynamic image analysis sensor from Sympatec, Germany used to determine particle size and shape distribution in various applications, including powders, granules, fibres, suspensions, and emulsions. When paired with a gravity dispersion system, such as the GRADIS, the QicPic can analyse coarse particles by utilizing a controlled drop chute for minimal dispersion, which is ideal for samples like granules. The system uses a high-resolution camera and pulsed LED to capture sharp images of falling particles, which are then evaluated by powerful algorithms to provide detailed and statistically significant particle size and shape distributions.

An experiment was conducted using QicPic sensor is used to determine the granule size distribution at different time points during kneading time. The granule size distribution at different time points are shown in **Figure 8.2**. Review of the granule size distributions at 30, 60, 90, 120, 150, 240 and 360 seconds indicates that except at 90 and 150 seconds, the granule size distribution at all other time points are bimodal, hence, these times are not able to provide uniform granules. Hence, subsequently two experiments are conducted with kneading time of 90 seconds and 150 seconds and both the granules were dried and evaluated and finally compressed into tablets and the tablets were also evaluated for hardness, DT and dissolution. The final results concluded that a kneading time of 150 seconds is suitable to achieve desired CQAs.

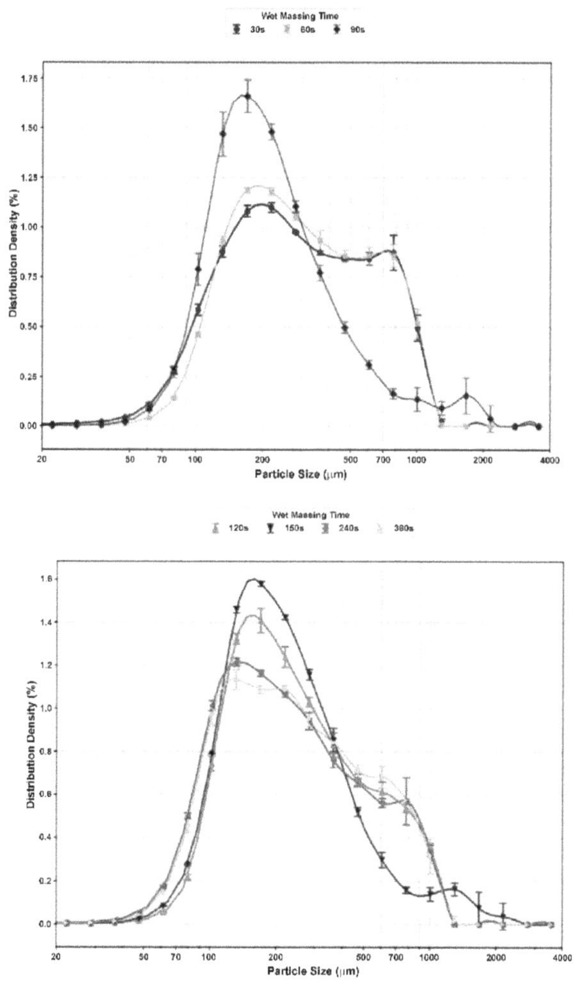

Figure 8.2 Granule size distribution at different time points of kneading.

How to carry out scale up trails has been explained using engineering principles and PAT tools for blending and wet granulation processes. Similarly, all other processes can be scaled up using these approaches.

Scale up based on Engineering Principles – Functional Film coating in Pan coater

The delayed release and controlled release tablets are developed by applying enteric materials or controlled release materials on to the tablets to form a continuous film with desired thickness. Pan coater is used for film coating of tablets. The process of film coating and the factors involved in the process must me understood thoroughly. **Figure 8.3** shows the schematic representation of Pan Coater.

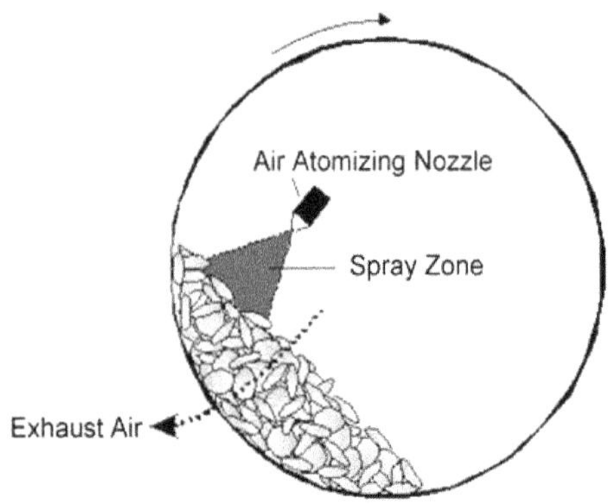

Figure 8.3 Schematic representation of Pan Coater.

The tablets to be coated are loaded into the pan and the pan is rotated at a particular speed that makes the tablets to roll in the pan. Air is flown in to the pan through small perforations in the bottom of pan and passes through the bed of tablets and into the exhaust port to outside. The inlet and out let temperature of the air are continuously measured and monitored. A spray gun is kept at a particular distance that sprays the coating liquid on to the tablets called spray zone. The spray rate and atomization pressure used determine the droplet size.

Once the coating process is initiated the tablets in the spray zone receive the coating liquid and new tablets come into the spray zone as the tablets are rolling. The coating process is continued until the desired percent of coating material is uniformly built on the surface of the tablets. Hence, tablet comes under spray zone and coating liquid droplets fall on to the surface and dries before it again reaches the spray zone. The tablet travels many numbers of times during coating process and continuously gains coating film uniformly till the desired percent build up is achieved.

Various process parameters that are critical for film coating in a pan coater are listed below.

Coating Pan Related

1. Pan Diameter
2. Pan speed
3. Pan depth
4. Pan brim volume
5. Pan load
6. Number of Guns

Tablets Related

1. Core Size
2. Core Shape

Spray Solution Related

1. Viscosity of Spray Solution
2. Surface Tension of Spray Solution

Spray Rate Related

1. Spray Rate
2. Inlet Airflow
3. Exhaust Air Temperature
4. Atomizing air pressure
5. Gun to Bed Distance
6. Spray Nozzle type and diameter
7. Coating Time

In product development stage, selection of Pan Coater leads to the fixed parameters related to Pan coater and the core tablets are selected from the lab scale development. Then the solution composition is finalized and its viscosity and surface tension are determined. The Critical Process Parameters are considered for the optimization using DoE and conducting required experiments. Finally, an optimized process with CPPs is used for the manufacture of film coated tablets at laboratory scale.

The scale up of coating process is initiated after establishing geometric, dynamic and kinematic similarity between lab scale and proposed Scale up size.

Geometric Similarity: Geometric similarity means that the shape and dimensions of the pan coater are proportional across various scales.

In order to keep the ratio of height (h) of the tablet bed to the diameter of the pan (D) constant, the pan load to pan volume ratio is kept constant across all scales.

$$\frac{\text{Pan Load}}{Pan\ Volume} = Constant \qquad .....(8.8)$$

Pan volume is typically the brim volume of the pan that is provided by the equipment supplier.

Dynamic Similarity: The ratio of forces at corresponding points in the pan coater has to be maintained constant across various scales to achieve dynamic similarity. The inertial and gravitational forces during the rotation of the pan have to be balanced to achieve a desirable motion of tablets. Imbalance in these two forces may lead to either sliding of tablets or turbulent flow of tablets. Balance of these two forces create a uniform flow of tablets in the pan during rotation. To achieve dynamic similarity between lab scale and scale up, Froude number (*Fr*) is kept constant across various scales.

$$Fr = \frac{\omega^2 * D}{g} \qquad .....(8.9)$$

Where ω is pan speed (RPM), D is the diameter of the pan and g is the gravitational constant.

Kinematic Similarity: Kinematic similarity ensures that the ratio of velocities (kinetics) at corresponding points in the pan is similar across scales. This can be achieved by keeping the velocity of tablets and spray kinetics constant. But the velocity of tablets changes as a function of the length along the cascading tablet bed. The next critical factor is the droplet size coming out of the spray gun. The droplet size in turn depends on nozzle type and size, atomising air, air pattern, spray rate and solution properties. The solution used at the lab scale is used in the scale up also and the nozzle type is also kept same. In order to achieve similar membrane morphology, the droplet size of the spray hitting the tablet should remain the same, provided that the tablets move at the same speed across scales. If T_{dry} is characteristic drying time for the droplet and $T_{surface}$ is the time the tablet spends on the bed surface, then for scale-up

$$\frac{\text{Tdry}}{\text{Tsurface}} = Constant \qquad .....(8.10)$$

However, it is difficult to get droplet size distribution and needs heavy experimentation. Therefore, in the absence of droplet size distribution data a macroscopic approach of the drying kinetics is employed.

Airflow

If the Airflow-to-spray rate, called drying capacity, and inlet temperature are held constant, the exhaust air temperature remains constant (Eq.8.11).

$$Drying\ capacity = \frac{\text{Airflow}}{\text{Spray Rate}} = Constant \quad .....(8.11)$$

Spray Rate

The tablets in spray zone get coating solution and then move to non-spray zone, comes back to the spray zone after some time, and during this time the drying of solution happens. Let us consider that '*n*' number of tablets present in the spray zone and total number of tablets in the pan are 'N', then the probability (*p*) of a tablet in spray zone is *n*/N. During the scale up both the pan load and spray area increase, but the increase in N (pan load) is many folds higher than that of *n*. Therefore, the probability of presence of tablet in the spray zone decreases. It means, it takes more time to come back to spray zone compared to smaller batch and this time is for drying of solution on tablet surface. The time between 2 successive coating events on a tablet is defined as the circulation time. Since more time is available for drying of solution in higher scale, higher spray rate can be used. Hence, the spray for scale up can be determined using the equation 8.12.

$$\frac{\text{Spray Rate}*n}{\text{N}} = Constant \quad .....(8.12)$$

It is possible to determine *n* value by measuring the spray zone area and surface area per tablet. Spray area divided by tablet surface area gives *n* value. The N value is calculated based on pan load. Total weight of tablets divided by one tablet weight.

In order to achieve high spray rate and keeping the microscopic spray zone similarity, either increase gun-to-bed distance, or increase atomizing air, or both. The distance between guns need to be adjusted based on the spray zone area covered by each gun.

Coating Time

Coating time decides the weight gain per tablet. The coating time required for scale up can be calculated using following equation.

$$\frac{\text{tcoat}*\text{Spray Rate}}{\text{Pan Load}} = Constant$$

This equation is used to calculate coating time by calculating the constant using the laboratory scale data.

The following **Table 8.3** shows the scale up calculations for process parameters for 52-inch pan coater based on 24-inch pan coater process parameters and the CQAs (weight gain, CV% and dissolution at 12 hours) (Table: 8.3). The calculations used for scale up are given below.

1. **Pan load:** $\frac{\text{Pan Load(L)}}{Pan\ Volume(L)} = \frac{\text{Pan Load(S)}}{Pan\ Volume(S)}$=14.5/30=Pan load(S)/225

Pan load(S) = 14.5*225/30=108.75 (rounded to **109** kgs)

"S" stands for scale up and "L" stands for lab scale

2. **Pan speed (rpm):** Froude number for lab scale = $(13)^2$*24/9.81= 413.456

   (Pan speed for Scale up)^2*52/9.81= 413.455

   Pan speed for Scale up = √(413.455*9.81)/52 = √78 = 8.831 (rounded to **9**)

3. **Spray rate:** The spray guns used in laboratory scale are 2 but 4 guns are proposed in scale up, hence, the spray area in scale up is 2 times that of lab scale. The total number of tablets are based on the pan load.

   Spray Rate for 52-inch Pan= (SR24)*(n24 /n52)*(N52/N24)=102* 2 (guns)*1/2*110/14.7=763 but 4 guns are used in scale up and hence, spray rate per gun = 763/4=190.8 (rounded to **191**).

4. **Airflow (L)/Spray rate (L)= Airflow (S)/Spray rate (S)**

   Airflow(S) = (Airflow (L)/Spray rate (L))*spray rate(S)= 200/204*764=749.019 (rounded to **750**)

Table 8.3 Scale Up process parameters calculated based on lab scale process parameters and the CQAs of coated tablets at lab and higher scales.

Process Parameters	**24-inch Pan Lab scale**	**52-inch Pan Scale Up**
Pan load (kg)	14.5	109
Pan speed (rpm)	13	9
Air flow (cu ft/min)	200	750
Spray rate (mL/min/gun)	102	191
Inlet temperature (°C)	50	50
Average membrane coat weight gain (mg/core)	*42*	*43.7*
Weight gain (coefficient of variation)	*4.6*	*5.2*
12-hour cumulative drug release (%)	*44.5±5.6*	*44.6 ± 1.3*

It can be seen from the data that the CQAs of the tablets are similar in both the scales. The scale up calculations based on engineering principles are highly useful in scale up of the process.

Scale up based on PAT tools – Film Coating in Pan Coater

In the example discussed under engineering principles-based scale up, the samples are analysed off-line and the data generated is reviewed. This methodology does not allow the understanding of the progress of the process. There are four types of sample analysis. They are in-line, on-line, at-line and off-line.

In-line means the measuring device is close proximity of sample and measurement is made. On-line measurement involves collection of sample and diversion from the main process, analysis and sample may return or may not. In case of at-line the sample is removed from the main process and analysed at the site immediately but the sample is lost. The off-line measurement is a routine activity where the sample is removed and sent for analysis away from the process site.

Most of the PAT tools utilize in-line, on-line and sometimes at-line measurements. Of all the methods, in-line measurement is immediate, fast and reflects process time. NIR spectroscopy, Terahertz, and Ram spectroscopy are best suited for in-line measurement of CQAs of a sample.

A coating process of film coating of core tablets with Hydroxypropyl Methyl Cellulose (HPMC) has to be monitored using PAT tools to gain information on weight gain of HPMC per tablet, uniformity of coat on tablet and moisture content of tablets since the coating is based on aqueous HPMC. Initially, IR spectra of core tablets reflects its composition and tracking of API IR spectrum is sufficient to track the coating build up. As the HPMC coats the tablet, the IR spectrum of HPMC starts appearing and the API related signals diminish. Analysis of the lab scale coated tablets with specific percent of build up by NIR allows the calibration of percent of HPMC versus the signal strength related to HPMC. This approach indicated the wavelength region from 5646 cm−1 to 5508 cm−1 as the best for the calculation HPMC coating growth based on tablet weight reference values. In addition, the water content of tablets can be monitored continuously. The most selective region for water was calculated in the wavelength range of 5492–4998 cm^{-1}.

A FT-NIR spectrometer is best suits for coating process because of its speed and spectra reproducibility. A FT-NIR spectrometer combined with a reflection-immersion probe in placed in the tablet bed. Addition ally, the system was equipped with a gas rinsing nozzle that enables cleaning of the optical window without removing the nozzle from the tablet bed. The arrangement of probe is shown in the **Figure 8.4**. The NIR diffuse reflectance spectra were collected from inside the rotating tablet bed of a pan coater. The NIR wavelength range used was 4000-12800cm^{-1} and in-line NIR spectra were continuously obtained for 10 tablets.

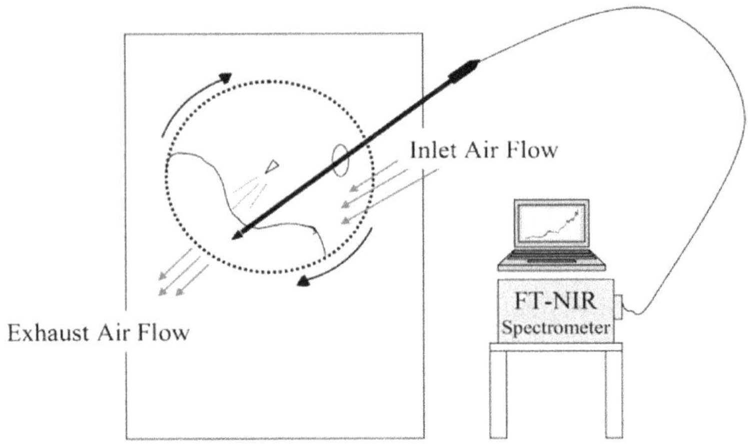

Figure 8.4 Schematic representation of location of NIR probe and FT-NIR Spectrophotometer.

The spectral data collected during the experiment by NIR spectrophotometer is analysed by multivariate method and suitable mathematical models are developed for monitoring HPMC and water contents during the process. **Figure 8.5A** shows the weight gain per tablet as per experimental data and predicted based on modelling with process time. **Figure 8.5B** shows the water content per tablet as per experimental data and predicted based on modelling with process time

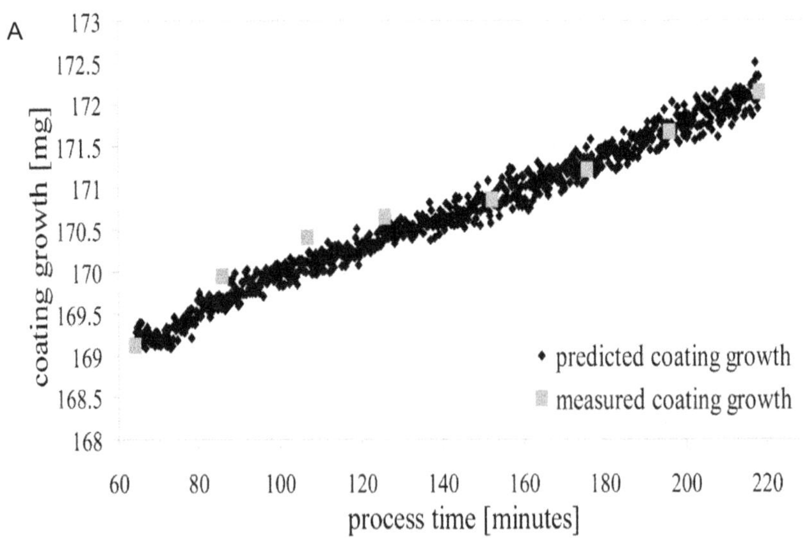

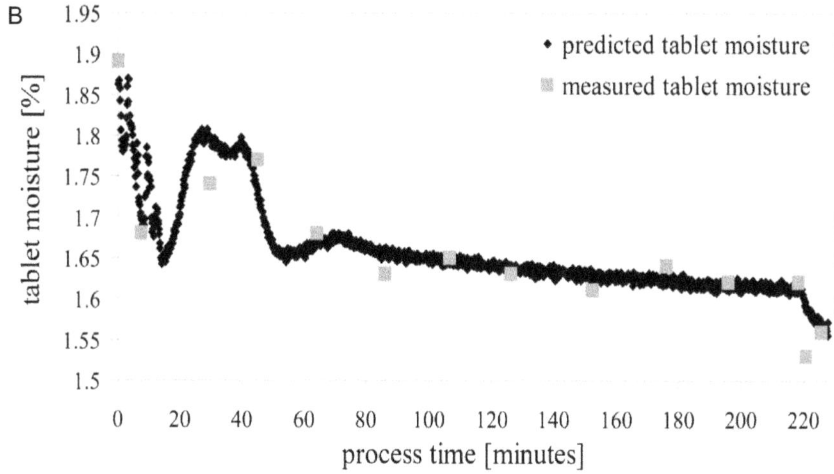

Figure 8.5 A-Process time versus weight gain per tablet and B-Process time versus water content per tablet.

It can be seen from the data that use of PAT tools such as NIR spectrophotometer enables continuous measurement of CQAs and the process can be stopped once the desired CQAs are achieved. This provides the flexibility of the process parameters adjustment to achieve desired quality in coated tablets.

CHAPTER 9

Control Strategy

As per the USFDA a control strategy "is a planned set of controls, derived from an in-depth understanding of the product and process, designed to ensure process performance and product quality." Hence, control strategy includes control of raw materials through specifications, defining quality target product profile, identification of critical material attributes (CMAs), critical process parameters (CPPs), process design, risk analysis, implementation of design of experiments (DoE), use of process analytical technology, scale up activities, creation of design space, controls on process parameters and monitoring of the process parameters during the manufacturing. Once the optimization of composition and process completes with design space, the controls for each

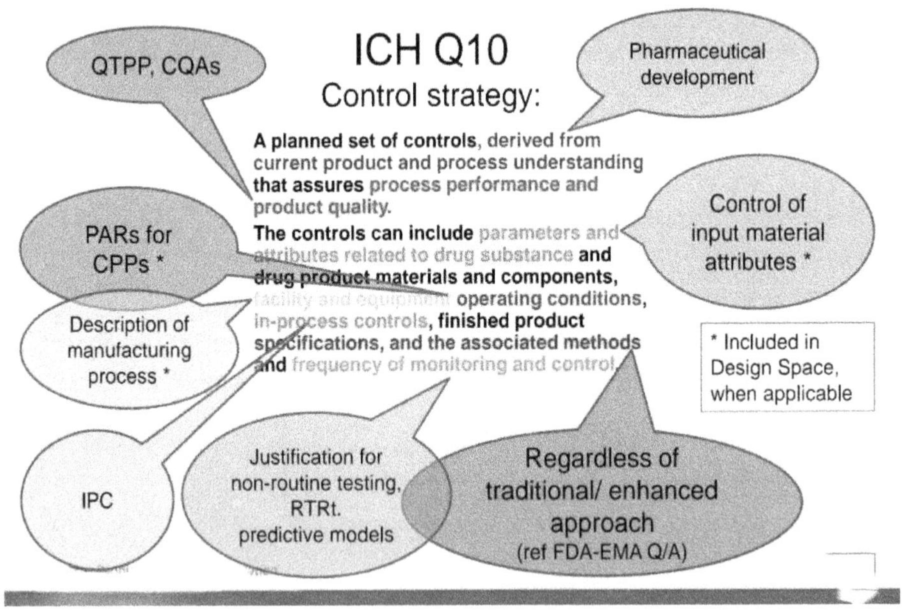

Figure 9.1 Control strategy and its components. PARs-proven acceptable ranges; IPC-intermediate process controls; RTRt- real time release tests.

critical process parameter is placed including CMAs. These controls would ensure the quality of drug product during the manufacturing of commercial batches. As discussed in previous chapters, the product and process understanding is achieved by conducting relevant experiments and analysing the data collected. Now proper controls have to be designed to ensure the production of dosage forms with defined quality attributes. ICH Q10 document clearly explains the control strategy and its significance. **Figure 9.1** depicts the components of control strategy related to its definition.

Strategic Controls

Strategic controls in a control strategy are a series of proactive measures and systematic checks, derived from product and process understanding, designed to ensure a desired quality and consistent performance of a process or product.

Derived from understanding

Controls are arrived based on a deep understanding of the raw material attributes, quantitative composition, process design and desired CQAs of the finished product. For example, the particle size distribution of API has a significance influence on dissolution profile of finished product and upon experimental verification a three-tier specification for D90, D50 and D10 is fixed as a control so that only those API lots that meet this specification are used in the manufacture of product. Similarly, a critical process parameter operational range is fixed based on the process understanding then the CPP has to be monitored within the proven acceptable range.

Systematic approach

A systematic approach to a control strategy is a structured, rules-based process for establishing controls that ensure consistent product quality and process performance.

Define clear, quantifiable, and realistic standards or targets that guide the entire manufacturing process. These standards are the reference for each batch manufactured and hence, data is collected for each batch and compared against the established standards to confirm the performance of the process and to identify any deviations or discrepancies. When deviations occur, document the event and correct the processes to ensure quality of product and build these learnings into the system by revising the controls or improving the process controls with advanced equipment. Efforts should be put to continuously improve the processes to make them more robust.

Proactive

Control strategy is proactive in nature not reactive. A control strategy builds quality into the process from the beginning, identifies issues via risk analysis and controls the issues early. In the traditional approach quality is focused on testing final product for critical quality attributes.

Assurance of Quality

Quality assurance (QA) in a control strategy involves the proactive, systematic processes and activities that a company implements to prevent defects and ensure that its products or services consistently meet predetermined quality standards and requirements.

Assurance of quality involves implementation of various activities, processes and reviews on regular basis. The management should commit for quality assurance and create a quality assurance department that works independently and reports to directly to top management to avoid any influence on their plans and execution. The QA personnel focus on the processes, methods, protocols, and procedures used to create a product. The employees are trained on quality systems of the organization, quality methodologies and processes. QA department responsibilities includes data collection, trend analysis, identification of improvement areas, revision of process controls and analytical methods. QA provides confidence to management, customers, and regulators that quality requirements will be met.

Integrated controls aim to centralize control, improve efficiency through automation and reduced manual intervention, and provide real-time data for better decision-making, ultimately leading to lower costs, increased reliability, scalability, and future-proofing of operations.

Materials

Specifications for drug substance and excipients are prepared with all the details of test to be performed and the acceptance criteria so that input materials quality is ensured. The specifications include physical, chemical, physiochemical, biological, microbiological and functional attributes. Primary and secondary packaging materials are also controlled through specifications to ensure product stability and usability.

Facility and Equipment

Facility and equipment refer to the physical assets of an organization – the buildings, structures, machinery, and tools – and their integrated management to ensure efficient, safe, and productive operations. A control strategy involving these elements focuses on asset management including preventive and predictive, capacity planning, safety protocols, and the strategic use of technology to monitor and optimize equipment performance, thereby reducing downtime, costs, and risks.

In-process Monitoring

In –process monitoring involves real-time observation, measurement, and analysis of critical process parameters (CPPs) and critical quality attributes (CQAs) to ensure a process operates within defined limits and consistently produces a high-quality product. Real-time data collection is done with sensors and automated systems and allows quick identification of deviations from desired performance and intervention to correct. This provides clear visibility of the process on-line and control of CPPs and CQAs. The methodology to monitor the controls and frequency at which the task to be performed.

Monitoring and Feedback

Monitoring and feedback are essential components of control strategy, where monitoring involves observing a system's performance against established standards, and feedback provides information about the output back to the system to enable adjustments and ensure objectives are met. This process, known as a closed-loop system, uses the discrepancy (error) between the desired and actual output to correct the system's behaviour, thereby enhancing its accuracy, stability, and overall effectiveness.

Monitoring allows for the measurement of key performance indicators (KPIs) and operational data. It detects deviations from the acceptable variations in a process parameter and provides current status of the system to the managers and controllers of the process to take appropriate decisions.

Feedback provides the necessary information to correct discrepancies between the desired and actual output, driving the system toward the desired state. Feedback allows systems to adapt to changing conditions and compensate for interruptions or external disturbances either automatically or by personal intervention.

Quality assurance is a journey for perfection that never ends. Hence, continuous learning, in depth understanding of the processes, introduction of new technologies, new methodologies to improve quality are essential components of quality assurance philosophy. It should be noted that drug products are for human consumption and failure to meet quality standards can even take lives of patients. Therefore, a commitment to highest quality in drug products is warranted without any compromise.

CHAPTER 10

Process Capability and Continuous Improvement

The purpose of process capability is to provide statistical data on performance, identify areas of poor quality, set a baseline for improvement, and reduce defects and costs. The purpose of continuous improvement is to use this data and other feedback to constantly refine processes, eliminate waste, enhance quality, and boost efficiency and profitability over time.

Process Capability

Let us understand the process and its performance. Each CQA has an allowed specification range that meets the quality standard and it is called specification width. For example, the acceptable assay value for API is given as 97% to 103% which is a specification width and it has lower specification limit (LSL) and upper specification limit (USL). The difference between USL and LSL is called specification width. The assay of API produced by a process is carried out for every batch and the values are recorded. The LSL and USL of the data generated for the batches are identified and the difference is called "process width" (**Figure 10.1a**). The process capability (Cp) is calculated by using equation 10.1.

$$Cp = \frac{\text{Specification Width}}{\text{Process With}} \quad .....(10.1)$$

It can be seen from the equation that only spread of the data is considered in the calculation of Cp.

It is always desired to produce API having an assay values close 100% and the spread should be low. It means the assay values should be very close to 100% with minimum variation. Hence, the mean should be 100% with less spread either side of the mean (**Figure 10.1b**). Process Capacity Index (Cpk) considers mean value and the nearest value to mean. In other words, Cpk considers the mean and spread of the data. The mean value of the specification and current process mean value are considered. The distance from mean to nearest specification limit and distance from mean to process edge are considered for the calculation of Cpk as per the equation 10.2.

$$\text{Cpk} = \frac{\text{Distance from mean to Nearest Spec Limit}}{\text{Distance from Mean to Process Edge}} \quad .....(10.2)$$

Cpk considers both the process's spread and its centering relative to the specification limits. A higher Cpk indicates a process that is both precise and accurate. If Cpk <1, the process is not capable and produces products outside the specifications. If Cpk≥1.33, the process is generally considered capable, indicating that virtually all product will fall within specifications. For new processes, a higher value like 1.5 is often targeted.

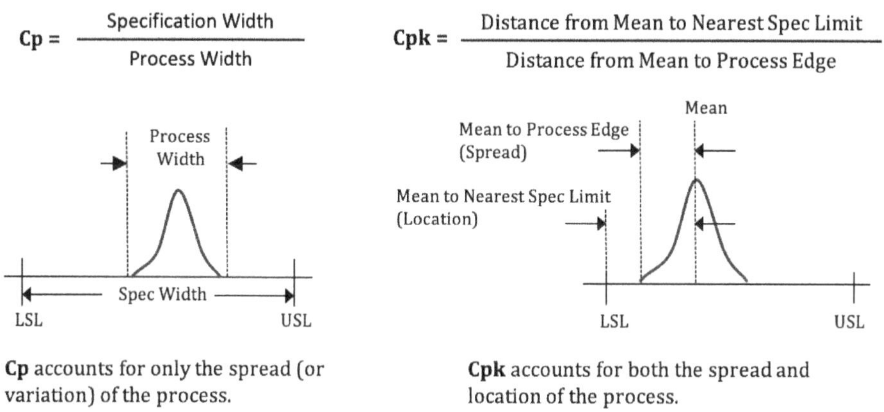

Figure 10.1(a)&(b) Process Capability (Cp) and Process Capability Index (Cpk).

Continuous Improvement

Continuous improvement in QbD is a core principle of quality assurance. A lifecycle approach where pharmaceutical manufacturers use data and knowledge to continuously refine and enhance product quality and manufacturing processes. The process is finalized after thorough experimentation and risk analysis during research and development and a design space is defined for the critical process parameters that produces quality product. In general, the centre of design space is used to manufacture the product continuously. However, in some batches, the CPP may deviate from the centre point but it is within design space may produce a dosage form having a particular CQA different from that obtained when the CPP is at the centre of design space. This provides a knowledge on how the CPP is influencing the CQA. The collection of such data for various batches manufactured with slight variation in CPPs and analysing their impact on CQAs would help in increase the process understanding and revision of CPPs within design space for improved quality of drug product. This process is followed continuously for the improvement of process and controls to achieve a robust manufacturing process for quality of dosage form.

CHAPTER 11

Quality by Design – Analytical Methods

Quality by design principles are not only applicable for formulation and process but also for analytical methods used to analyse API, excipients, intermediates and finished product. The QbD approach for analytical method development and validation is similar to the one discussed in previous chapters. ICH guidelines Q12 and Q14 provide the details of analytical method development, validation, control strategy, continuous improvement and lifecycle management of analytical method and also change control. The essential components of QbD in analytical method development are listed below.

1. Analytical Target Profile (ATP)
2. Critical Method Attributes (CMAs)
3. Critical Method Parameters (CMPs)
4. Risk Assessment (ICH Q9)
5. Design of Experiments (DoE)
6. Method Operable Design Region (MODR)
7. Control Strategy
8. Lifecycle Management (ICH Q12 & Q14)

The very purpose of an analytical method is to measure critical method attributes of sample and the method used should be robust to give reproducible results. The analytical methods used in pharmaceutical industry range from simple gravimetric to highly advanced process analytical tools. Regardless of the method sophistication, every method should be developed, optimized and validated using same set of scientific principles and steps. HPLC is the most prominent analytical instrument used in pharmaceutical industry for the measurement many of the critical quality attributes of API, excipients and finished dosage forms. Therefore, this chapter focuses on analytical method development and validation using HPLC.

HPLC analytical method essentially consist of a column, mobile phase, separation procedure, detection, and analysis of eluted peaks in chromatogram. A sample is analysed for a specific characteristic that is an essential desired quality.

1. **Analytical Target Profile (ATP):** Analytical Target Profile (ATP) is similar to QTPP of drug product and an ATP consists of a description of the intended purpose, appropriate details on the product attributes to be measured and relevant performance characteristics with associated performance criteria. Let us consider quantification of a drug in a tablet. The purpose is to develop a method that estimates drug content in tablet quantitatively. The performance criteria are an accuracy of $\pm 2\%$, limit of quantification of 0.4 ug/ml and precision is RSD$\leq$2%. The ATP facilitates the selection of the technology, the procedure design and development as well as the subsequent performance monitoring and continual improvement of the analytical procedure.
2. **Critical Method Attributes (CMAs):** Critical method attributes (CMAs) are measurable outputs of the analytical method that assure the performance of the analytical method and these outputs are linked to ATP. The CMAs Include accuracy, precision, specificity, sensitivity, linearity, robustness, detection/quantification limits. In addition, resolution between the closely eluting peaks can be considered as CMA. Identification of CMAs of the analytical method is critical since the decisions for further studies depends on these criteria.
3. **Critical Method Parameters (CMPs):** Critical method parameters are similar to critical process parameters in manufacturing process of drug product. These are the factors that impact CMAs and hence, need to be identified, studied and optimised to achieve desired output. The examples of CMPs are pH, mobile phase composition, column temperature, wavelength, flow rate, injection volume. These input factors can be modified at will by the analytical scientists. All the method parameters have to be listed first and then the critical method parameters have to be identified with previous knowledge, literature and risk assessment.
4. **Risk Assessment (ICH Q9):** The risk assessment, analysis and communication are discussed in detail in the product development. Similar tools and techniques are applicable for analytical method development. The risk assessment and analysis should not only identify CMPs but have to be prioritized based on the risk priority number (RPN). If the number of CMPs are more, a screening design may be useful in identifying the most significant CMPs that can be further studies and optimized.
5. **Design of Experiments (DoE):** A detailed information has been provided on this topic in previous chapters which can be applied here. After analysis of experimental data from screening design, the significant CMPs are

further subjected for multivariate study to understand their effect on CMAs. A design space that is a multidimensional region where method performance is assured has to be established.

6. **Method Operable Design Region (MODR):** The operational range for each CMP is established that provides regulatory flexibility during analysis. Changes within MODR do not require re-approval of regulatory agency since the change is not treated as deviation. For example, the operable range for pH is 5.0 - 6.5 then any pH used within this range is not a deviation but within the proven acceptable range.
7. **Control Strategy:** The essential feature of control strategy is to set controls that ensure that the method remains within MODR. For example, system suitability tests, column control, instrument calibration, etc. are used to ensure that the method is within the MODR.
8. **Lifecycle Management (ICH Q12 & Q14):** Lifecycle management is beyond the method validation and involves continuous monitoring and method performance verification. The data collected from several samples analysis and standards is subjected for trend analysis such as control charts to ensure method robustness. If modification of a CMP or CMPs operation range is required, then it is made effective via change management as detailed in ICH Q14.

Case Study

Analytical target profile (ATP) is the first step in method development using QbD principles. The critical method attributes (CMAs) have to be defined with clear cut acceptance criteria. The CMAs differ based on the analytical method under development such as assay method, dissolution method or related substances (RS) also known as impurities analytical method etc.

Ishikawa diagram is often used to identify the critical method parameters. **Figure 11.1**is a useful starting point for the identification of CMPs.

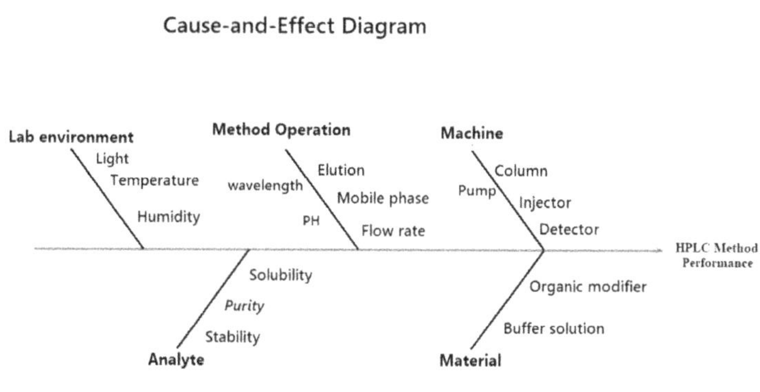

Figure 11.1 Ishikawa diagram for the identification of CMPs.

Table 11.1 shows some examples of CMAs based on analytical method but the actual CMAs for targeted analytical method have to be selected carefully. The critical analysis of the factors from Ishikawa diagram and scientific rationale are used to identify the CMAs and CMPs.

Table 11.1 CMAs for some analytical methods.

Method	Tailing Factor	%RSD	Plate Counts	Recovery	Run time	Resolution
Assay	NMT 2.0	NMT 2.0	NLT 2000	97%-103%	<15 min	No interference at main peak
RS	NMT 1.5	NMT 10%	NLT 2000	85%-115%	<60 min	NLT 1.5
Dissolution	NMT 2.0	NMT 2.0	NLT 2000	95%-105%	<10 min	No interference at main peak

Critical method parameters (CMPs) are the input variables that have an impact on the CMAs. Hence, the CMPs have to be optimized to meet the acceptance criteria of CMAs. For example, pH of buffer, concentration of buffer, organic modifier in mobile phase, diluent for sample preparation, sonication time etc.

Risk Assessment of the assay method development is considered here. Let us consider the method development for assay of a drug in immediate release tablets. The CMPs and CMAs are identified after thorough risk analysis and are presented in **Table 11.2.**

Table 11.2 CMPs, CMAs and their acceptance criteria for assay of drug in tablets by HPLC.

CMPs	CMAs	Acceptance Criteria for CMAs
Methanol % in mobile phase	Tailing factor	NMT 2.0
pH of mobile phase	%RSD	NMT 2.0
Flow rate (ml/min)	Plate counts	NLT 2000
Temperature °C	Recovery	97%-103%
Wavelength	Run time	<15 min
	Resolution between peaks	NLT 2.0

Design of Experiments by Design Expert® software using fraction factorial design for screening of CMPs to identify the impact on CMAs is carried out. The number of factors is 5 and the levels are 2. A full factorial design gives 32 experiments (2^5) but the fractional factorial design provides 16 experiments that would be sufficient for screening of factors. The factors and their low and high levels are provided in **Table 11.3**.

Table 11.3 The two levels of CMPs selected for DoE.

CMPs	Low	High
Methanol % in mobile phase	75	85
pH of mobile phase	2.5	3.5
Flow rate (ml/min)	1.0	1.4
Temperature °C	25	30
Wavelength	240	250

All the 16 experiments were conducted as per run order the responses (CMAs) for each experiment were recorded. A Pareto analysis of the data for all CMAs has shown that flow rate, methanol % and pH have significant impact on the CMAs whereas temperature and wavelength have negligible impact. Hence, further optimization of 3 factors at 2 levels is considered and full factorial design is considered. The number of experiments for full factorial design is 2^3=8 and 3 central points were included to estimate variation and hence, a total of 11 experiments were conducted. The CMAs identified were resolution between peaks and run time. The assay method should meet the specificity criteria with proper resolution between the main peak and other impurities. HPLC resolution (Rs) measures peak separation, calculated by dividing the difference in retention times (Δt_R) by the average peak width. **Table11.4** shows the experiments, CMPs and CMAs.

Table 11.4 Experiments based on fractional factorial design.

Run	pH	Organic solvent %	Flow Rate ml/min	RS1	RS2	Run Time
1	-1	1	-1	8.08	6.82	6.28
2	0	0	0	7.80	6.88	6.06
3	1	-1	1	9.50	7.53	6.46
4	-1	1	1	6.69	5.35	4.93
5	0	0	0	7.60	6.80	6.06
6	0	0	0	7.60	6.81	6.06
7	1	-1	-1	10.23	9.13	8.72
8	1	1	1	6.40	6.26	4.88
9	-1	-1	-1	10.19	9.27	8.59
10	-1	-1	1	9.51	8.34	6.47
11	1	1	-1	6.83	7.07	6.29

RS1 = Resolution between main peak and impurity 1 and RS2 = Resolution between main peak and impurity 2.

Conduct of Experiments

The experiments were conducted as per the Run order and the CMAs (RS1, RS2 and Runt time) were captured for each experiment. The data obtained is analysed using the DoE software. The main effect plots are shown in **Figure 11.2a, b &c** for RS1, RS2 and Run Time respectively.

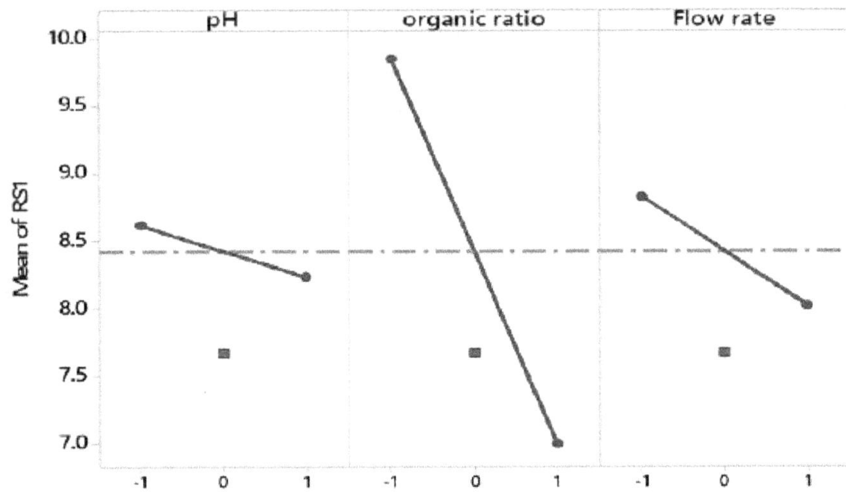

Figure 11.2(a) Main effects plot for RS1 (Fitted means).

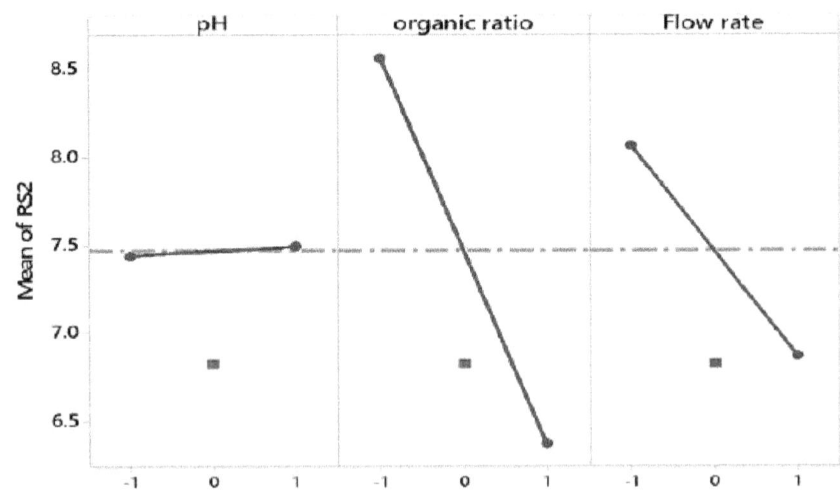

Figure 11.2(b) Main effects plot for RS2 (Fitted means).

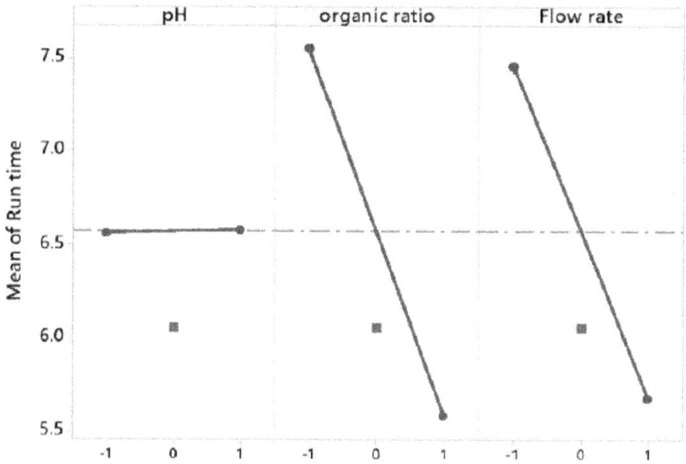

Figure 11.2(c) Main effects plot for Run Time (Fitted means).

The main effects plots show the effect of each variable on the CMAs. An interaction plots of CMPs on CMAs were also analysed and found that there is no significant interaction between the CMPs. The responses were fitted into the mathematical model and the equations for each CMA are given below.

RS1 is the resolution between impurity one and the parent drug. The mathematical equation that describes the relation between RS1, RS2, Run time and the input variables are given below.RS1 = 1.22 + 0.211 pH - 0.22 methanol - 0.07 flow rate - 0.014 pH*flow rate - 0.03*pH*methanol - 0.098 flow rate*methanol - 0.26 pH*methanol*flow rate .....(11.1)

RS2 = 24.19 - 8.58 pH - 9.24methanol - 14.2*flow rate - 2.10 pH*flow rate + 2.9*pH*methanol+5.09 pH*methanol + 6.85 pH*methanol*flow rate .....(11.2)

Run time = 2.54 - 0.022 pH + 0.25 methanol + 0.015 flow rate - 0.14 pH*flow rate+ 0.28 pH*methanol + 0.18 pH*methanol*flow rate .....(11.3)

Now it is possible to predict the CMAs by varying the CMPs and the operable method parameters can be determined before proceeding to the validation of analytical method.

The QbD approach using DoE results in an analytical method that has been studied scientifically, subjected for risk analysis and allows informed decision making. The creation of design space or method operable design region allows the pharmaceutical industries to change the CMPs within the region without prior approval from regulatory agencies and provides robust analytical method that is flexible for adjustment of CMPs for accurate results.

www.ingramcontent.com/pod-product-compliance
Lightning Source LLC
Chambersburg PA
CBHW071225230926
51849CB00001B/25
* 9 7 8 9 3 4 7 3 1 1 4 0 6 *